D1295146

MEDAL
of
HONOR
HEROES

Here are the remarkable stories of some of America's great war heroes—men who have won their country's highest military decoration, the Medal of Honor. Chosen from among the veterans of two World Wars, as well as the War in Korea, these men all earned their Medals in the only way this highly honored decoration can be won: by a deed of personal bravery or self-sacrifice above and beyond the call of duty. Sergeant York, Audie Murphy, Father O'Callahan, Butch O'Hare, and General William Dean are but five of the outstanding Americans whose exciting and inspiring deeds are recorded in this book.

MEDAL
of
HONOR
HEROES

by Colonel Red Reeder

Illustrated by Gil Walker

RANDOM HOUSE ● New York

FOR:

Virginia Martin Riggs

Dale Eugene Hruby II

Dorothea Lee Hruby

Philip Russell Riggs

Alan Johnstone McCutchen II

Elizabeth Mae Hruby

Dorothea Darrah Riggs

Contents

PART THREE: *The War in Korea: 1950–1953*

The Medal

The story of America's most honored military decoration—the Medal of Honor—begins with the Civil War. When the War Between the States started, certain government leaders saw the need for recognizing deeds of men who were *extraordinarily brave* in combat. An Iowan, Senator James W. Grimes, introduced a bill to create a Navy Medal. Both Houses of Congress passed the bill and Abraham Lincoln signed it in 1861.

The Army Medal was established two months later when Senator Henry Wilson of Massachusetts introduced a resolution providing "medals of honor" for enlisted men of the Army and Voluntary Forces who "shall distinguish themselves by gallantry in action." This was followed by a phrase that would later cause difficulty: *"and other soldier-like qualities."*

President Lincoln's approval made the resolution a law, and the wording was soon expanded to include officers. The correct name of the award is "The Medal of Honor," although it may be called "The Congressional Medal of Honor" because it is awarded by Act of Congress.

At first, the Medal was slow to be awarded; then it was given out in quantities. During the Civil War approximately 2,100 Medals of Honor were awarded. More than three hundred of these were won by sailors or marines. By today's standards this was extremely generous. In World War II, when more than twelve million United States soldiers, sailors, and airmen served in the armed forces, only 292 Medals of Honor were presented. In the Civil War, however, there was one instance in which every man in a regiment from Maine was given the Medal for work *behind* the Union lines. When the Civil War era ended, and officials realized that the Medal had been awarded almost promiscuously, approximately nine hundred of the Medals of Honor were revoked.

Today, if an entire unit performs in an unusually outstanding manner, its members may be awarded the Distinguished Unit Citation, a blue ribbon rimmed in gold and worn on the right breast of a uniform. For heroism in action against the enemy, individuals may receive the Bronze Star, the Silver Star, the Navy Cross, the Distinguished Service Cross, and—hardest of all to win—the Medal of Honor. The Medal may be earned in only one way: by a deed of personal bravery or self-sacrifice *above and beyond the call of duty*. The winner's act must be witnessed by at least two reliable witnesses, and it must involve the risk of the hero's life. He must be a member of the United States Armed Forces, and his action must be in combat against an enemy of the United States. Or he may win the Medal while serving with friendly foreign forces in combat against an opposing armed force. (There are instances on record in which exceptions have been made. Charles A. Lindbergh and a very few others have been awarded the Medal as a result of special Congressional action.) The deed that wins the Medal must be one which, if it were left undone, would bring no criticism against the doer. To win the Medal of Honor a man must do far more than is expected.

The tremendous value of the Medal rests in the respect its wearer commands by holding the nation's highest decoration. General Dwight D. Eisenhower, when he was chief of staff of the Army, once said of the Medal of Honor, "I would rather have the right to wear it than be President of the United States."

This is the only United States decoration that brings any accompanying award. Under certain conditions, Medal of Honor men may obtain free rides on military planes. Their military pay, if they are enlisted men, is increased by $2.00 a month, and the recipient is usually entitled to a pension of $100 a month after he reaches the age of fifty-six.

Since the Medal of Honor has been in existence, Congress has awarded it 2,200 times. This figure includes five awards to soldiers who received the Medal twice and ten Medals awarded by special acts of Congress to the Unknown Soldiers of the United States and various foreign countries, and to such public figures as Major General Adolphus W. Greeley, arctic explorer, and Charles A. Lindbergh for outstanding noncombat achievements.

Because the standards for awarding the Medal have been higher since 1900, and because the individual military records have been more complete, this book is devoted exclusively to twentieth century heroes of the highly coveted Medal of Honor.

PART ONE

World War I
1914-1918

1

LIEUTENANT IZAC
and His Escape

In 1914 the First World War broke out in Europe. This conflict was to develop into the worst war the world had yet seen, and it would touch the lives of people all over the globe.

The causes of the war were far from simple. Defeat in the Franco–Prussian War of 1870 had humiliated an unforgiving France. Then when Germany began to rival other nations for markets in Africa, Asia, and the islands of the Pacific, the other powers began to look on her with jealousy and suspicion. Germany's overseas expansion, buttressed by a rapidly growing navy, alarmed political leaders in Great Britain. They saw Germany as a threat to the British Empire. Nor could they derive any comfort from the fact that the Kaiser Wilhelm, Germany's emperor, dreamed of militaristic glory. He saw himself as a shining leader destined to place his country in the front rank of world power.

The masses of Europeans, however, were not aware of the intrigues and rivalries in high places. Consequently they were surprised when Austria, with the backing of Germany, blamed Serbia for the assassination of Austria's Archduke Francis Ferdinand and issued an ultimatum that led to a declaration of war. Soon Germany and Austria were fighting the Allies— France, England, and Russia—with many other countries joining the fray.

When huge German armies violated the neutrality of Belgium and crashed through that small country in 1914, most Americans felt angry. But at the same time it seemed inconceivable that the war could reach across the Atlantic and embroil the United States.

By April of 1917, however, the United States was finally drawn into the conflict, partly as a result of ruthless German submarine warfare and partly because of propaganda spread by the hard-pushed Allies. In spite of the country's desire to be of immediate aid, it took a year for the United States to develop and train her forces. The country had plunged into war although by European standards she lacked an army and an air force. She did have the third largest navy in the world, but her fleet lacked officers and men and needed battle practice.

The gigantic task of preparing to join the fight on

the other side of the Atlantic was grim, but few Americans contemplated the morbid aspects. Instead, enthusiasm and determination marked the effort to get ready for the conflict.

Finally, in 1918, the United States Navy began the tremendous task of transporting the American army overseas. Of tremendous concern were the German U-boats. In just the month of April, 1917, enemy submarines had sunk almost one million tons of shipping.

To defeat the undersea raiders, the United States Navy grouped transports and supply ships heading for France into convoys and protected them with warships. This practice was so successful that not a single one of the two million soldiers traveling to Europe was lost. But the return trips were a different story, for seldom were enough men-of-war available to protect the empty ships from the sharklike submarines.

On May 29, 1918, the *President Lincoln* and three sister ships steamed away from England, heading for New York for another load of soldiers. The *Lincoln* carried no cargo, but her crew numbered over five hundred sailors and about five hundred naval officers. In command of the guns on the afterdeck was First Lieutenant Edouard Victor M. Izac.

At first American and French destroyers patrolled alongside the four liners, but on the thirtieth of May they signaled that they were leaving to carry out other

orders. The four merchant ships sailing west into the
long swells of the Atlantic doubled their lookouts and
steamed on alone. Seven hours after the destroyers had
disappeared over the horizon, the lookouts saw what
they dreaded most: two thousand yards behind them
the periscope of a German submarine peered above
the water.

The liners turned on all the steam their boilers
could carry and zigzagged frantically, but the submarine hung on. When night came, a full moon illumi-
nated her targets.

The German skipper studied the irregular course
of the four ships and, after a few hours, was able to
determine their true course. He submerged and made
a wide detour beneath the waves that carried him miles
ahead. There he waited quietly under the surface in

ambush. A newly invented underwater listening device told the submarine captain when his quarry was in the right place. At nine in the morning he ran up his scope. The *President Lincoln* was steaming by, inky-black in a light fog. The sub slammed three torpedoes into her.

Huge columns of water shot into the air as the torpedoes exploded against the *Lincoln.* Her sister ships hurried from the scene, for they lacked weapons to battle the raider.

In ten minutes the *Lincoln* began to sink at the stern, and her captain, seeing that his ship was lost, gave the fateful order, "Abandon ship!" His well-drilled crew lowered lifeboats, slid down ropes into them, and pulled away. Within an hour the *Lincoln* stood upended on her stern and disappeared in a lonely farewell scene.

The *Lincoln's* crew rowed for England, the little boats riding the waves like so many chips. Alongside the dismal formation chugged the enemy submarine, looking like a sleek, black shark, except for the blue exhaust smoke wreathing its stern. Fountains of spray sloshing against the German sub made the symbol on her conning tower, *U-90,* glisten.

Officers on the bridge of the sub questioned the men
in each lifeboat until they came to Lieutenant Izac.
They knew by the gold braid on his coat that young
Izac was an officer, so they took him aboard the submarine as a prisoner.

In the cramped little control room, Captain Remy,
skipper of the *U-90*, saluted the American and said in
perfect English, "My orders are to take prisoner the
senior officer on each ship that we sink. Where is your
captain?"

Lieutenant Izac said, "He went down with the ship."
(Actually the commanding officer of the *Lincoln* was
in another lifeboat and escaped capture.)

The skipper of the *U-90* gave Izac the run of the
submarine, and the American lieutenant spent hours
studying her. He gathered valuable information about
German submarine construction, the depth at which
the *U-90* usually cruised, the depth to which she could
descend without straining her plates, and her speed

above and below the surface. He also learned where she and other German submarines patrolled, the maximum number of days they could stay away from their mother ship, *Preussen,* and the area where the mother ship cruised. He even found out what routes the submarines took when traveling from interception areas to their base at Wilhelmshaven, Germany.

The American was obsessed with the idea of getting this information to officials in the United States Navy. It would enable the Allied navies to trap and sink numbers of submarines. The lieutenant vowed never to rest until he had delivered the information.

Since there was no way to send the information back, it was clear that he must escape—but how? He thought his chance had come when the *U-90* was cruising the black waters of a little bay between Sweden and Denmark on the way back to her base. Both Sweden and Denmark had remained neutral, and Izac thought if he could swim ashore he might find people who would help him. He was getting ready to jump when the submarine captain stopped him and sent him below.

At Wilhelmshaven, Izac was placed in a solitary cell for several days. Then a German who spoke English was locked in with him, and hours of questioning began. The German quizzed the American about the United States Navy and its methods of transporting men and supplies, but the American refused to talk. Clearly he would be helping the enemy if he did. He had discovered a tiny dictaphone hidden in the cell, ready to record any secrets he might reveal.

When the Germans learned that Lieutenant Izac was loyal and careful, they placed him on a train bound for the prison camp at Villingen, Germany. The train was rattling along at forty miles an hour when Izac heard a guard say that they would be at Villingen prison in a few minutes. Izac decided that he would have a better chance of escaping from the train than from a prison. The guard nearest him was half asleep; others farther back in the swaying coach were paying little attention. Suddenly the American stood up and dived through a glass window, no larger than eighteen inches by twenty-four inches. He struck his head on one of the steel ties. His knees were badly cut by another tie. He lay stunned while the brakes of the train ground, bringing the train to a stop.

When Izac finally managed to pull himself to his feet, the train was at a standstill three hundred yards down the track. Three guards were running toward him. The lieutenant tried to run, but a guard knelt, aimed, and sent a stream of bullets past Izac's shoulder. The American stopped, threw up his hands, and surrendered.

The German guards were infuriated because he had attempted escape. One German beat the runaway over the head with the barrel of his gun and, when Izac went down, all three kicked him. Another guard walloped Izac with his gun until it broke at the stock. When Izac fainted, they stopped beating him. But as soon as he regained consciousness, they began again. Finally they jerked him to his feet and double-timed him to the prison camp, five miles down the track. They took pleasure in punching and kicking him.

Izac was thrown into a cell infested with bugs and, although the prison doctor cared for him, three days passed before he could stand up. He was hauled before a court-martial, sentenced to fourteen days in solitary confinement, and warned that if he ever attempted to escape again he would be shot.

When Izac finished his lonely confinement, he was thirty pounds lighter, weighing only one hundred and twenty pounds. But in spite of his bad physical condition and repeated warnings that he would face a firing squad if he tried to escape, he decided to take the chance. He figured that his information about submarines was worth the risk of losing his life.

The chance of escape did not appear promising because the prison camp was surrounded by a deep ditch with a barbed-wire fence running along its bottom, projecting four feet above ground. On the far side stood another barbed-wire fence ten feet high, its top wires curving inward to prevent anyone from climbing over. Outside the fence walked a chain of sentries, one every thirty yards, and inside the prison camp two more sentries patrolled. Escape seemed impossible, but Izac was determined to risk it.

Several times he worked out plans to flee the prison, but every attempt was blocked. He came to the conclusion that some Russian officers who were also prisoners were relaying his plans to the prison commandant.

On the morning of October 6, Lieutenant Izac called a secret meeting of twelve American officers who were fellow prisoners. Each had assured him that he wanted to escape, and Izac explained his latest plan. He and his twelve friends would divide into four teams, each team with an escape scheme of its own. All four plans would be put into operation at the same time.

That afternoon Izac and two American aviators on his team stole a file, an iron chain, and a section of a wooden backstop from an old tennis court, smuggling the articles inside the barrack. Then they went to work sawing the window bars of their cell with the file.

At 10:30 P.M., soon after the lights were out, Izac and his men threw the stolen chain over the electric light wires. By yanking on it, they short-circuited the wires, putting the lights out. Then they bent aside the damaged bars at the window and ran the backstop out the window to the fence on the far side of the ditch, making a bridge. When this bridge struck the fence, the guards discovered it and fired. Izac and his team-mates crawled out the window, crossed the bridge, dropped beside the guards, and ran. The guards fired again, but in the darkness they missed. One sentry fired his gun almost in Izac's face.

Part of the third team, which rushed the main gate after some of the guards there had been called away in the confusion to help at other places, succeeded in getting away. One man from this group, Lieutenant

Harold B. Willis, a pilot in the Lafayette Escadrille, joined Izac at a planned rendezvous, two miles away.

Although Izac and his little group were not in good physical condition, they traveled on foot 120 miles in six days. They were certain that the reserve battalion of prison guards, three hundred strong, would soon be chasing them with bloodhounds. The fugitives walked in icy streams to throw the hounds off the scent, through underbrush, through forests, over mountains, and across country. They had no food except vegetables they stole from the fields. When they reached what they thought would be their last barrier, the Rhine River, they found German soldiers patrolling its banks. Freedom seemed as far away as ever.

For four long hours Izac and his men crawled about in the bushes, trying to get by the patrols. Finally, the escaped prisoners were able to crawl unobserved into a stream that emptied into the Rhine. They peeled off most of their clothes and entered the river.

The swim across the Rhine was frightening because of the strong current and the freezing water. The water numbed them, and the current separated the men. Izac battled the current for ten minutes until he was exhausted, then floated downstream until he crashed against some rocks. The rocks hurt, but they were within the boundaries of Switzerland. The little group had landed near Laufenburg.

When Lieutenant Izac had gained strength to struggle ashore, he walked to a farmhouse. Here a kindly Swiss fed and clothed him and summoned the police. The friendly Swiss police had already located Lieutenant Willis three miles away.

In Berne, Switzerland, the American legation helped Lieutenants Izac and Willis to leave the country, and the American Red Cross lent them money so they could travel to Paris. Finally, on October 23, 1918, the invincible Edouard Izac realized his dream. On that day he reported to Admiral William S. Sims, commander of the United States Naval Force in Europe, and gave him very valuable information to help defeat the enemy submarines.

After the war, Commander Izac was elected to Congress from California and served four terms. Now retired, he lives in Washington, D.C. (when he is not traveling) and devotes his spare time to writing. He was one of twenty-eight Navy men who won the Medal of Honor in the First World War.

2

OSCAR SCHMIDT,
Rescue at Sea

One of the most intriguing enterprises of the First World War was the employment of small surface craft, dubbed "submarine chasers," against German U-boats. Destroyers were even more dangerous enemies of the subs, but when the United States entered the war, the destroyers were needed to protect convoys carrying troops.

Thus the tiny submarine chasers, measuring only 110 feet from bow to stern and displacing but 77 tons, performed valuable work along the coast of Europe. They provided diminutive targets for a submarine's guns; they were almost too little to be hit by a torpedo. And in small fleets, working against the submarines, they could rain showers of depth bombs on the underwater enemy. However, the wooden sub chasers had a serious defect: because of their lack of size they could carry only enough gasoline for a nine-hundred-mile cruise.

The United States built almost four hundred chasers in the first eighteen months of the war, and solved the problem of cruising them to Europe by sending along a fuel tanker with each flotilla of sub chasers. This solution was less foolproof than it sounded, for the little ships were difficult to fuel when the Atlantic was not placid. And there was also danger of fire when the fuel flowed through the lines.

One of the thousands of Navy men sailing on the high seas to combat the submarine menace was Oscar Schmidt, Jr., twenty-two-year-old chief gunner's mate on the tanker *Chestnut Hill*.

As a boy Schmidt had lived in an old residential area of Philadelphia called "Fish Town," approximately a mile north of the center of the city. For recreation he went swimming in the Delaware River. As his family

was poor, he had to leave school at the age of fourteen and go to work. The job he obtained, that of apprentice machinist, was virtual slavery; he labored in a small machine shop, and in return for a 55-hour week received $3.25. Young Schmidt soon bettered his pay by obtaining work in the Philadelphia Shipyard, and there he got the urge to follow the sea.

When he was seventeen and a half, Schmidt obtained his parents' permission to enlist and presented himself at a United States Navy Recruiting Station. But the doctor snorted when the would-be sailor stepped on the scales. Schmidt, five feet six inches tall, weighed but a feather over 108 pounds.

"The minimum weight is 110 pounds," the doctor said. "I advise you to go out and take aboard all the water you can drink, and eat a cargo of bananas."

In three hours Schmidt was back. He made the weight with a half-pound to spare.

Schmidt proved he was an able, quick learner, and the seamen serving with him liked his sense of humor and his friendly nature. No young sailor had more eagerness or confidence than this young featherweight with the turned-up nose. In a period of just four years he was promoted five times, and when the United States declared war he was placed in command of the three-inch guns aboard the *Chestnut Hill*.

In late September, 1918, the big tanker, unwieldy because of her load of gasoline, sailed from Bermuda on a course of 75 degrees for the Azores.

Hovering about the *Hill,* like chicks about a hen, was a flotilla of seventy-five submarine chasers. The chasers were manned by Americans, Frenchmen, and Italians, few of whom had ever followed the sea. Some were college boys. On the outskirts of the flotilla of little ships, a mile out, two destroyers, on loan from convoy duty, guarded the fleet to see that no underwater shark swallowed a "chick."

Whitecaps dotted the blue water as Bermuda receded into the distance, finally fading from sight over the horizon. Hazy gray smoke wreathed the stern of each sub chaser as the gasoline motors chugged away. Spray flew over the sterns, low in the water, and doused the Y-guns and depth charges glistening in the sun. A three-inch gun was mounted on the bow of each tiny vessel, but the Y-guns, depth charges, and K-tube fish hydrophones were the equipment the crews depended upon to defeat the U-boats. The hydrophones could detect the whir of a sub's propellers within an acoustic radius of almost one thousand yards, and each Y-gun could fire two depth charges at a time. The depth charges looked like ash cans, and that was, in fact, their nickname. They contained TNT powder that could cave in a submarine's hull if exploded close to the underwater boat.

The voyage east was difficult. Refueling in rough weather was a dangerous task that no one liked. A schedule devised to stagger the times for refueling worked the crew of the *Chestnut Hill* long hours. The sub chasers, each with a crew of fourteen, had enough men for routine watches and to man the gasoline engines, but rough weather rolled the little vessels as if they were miniatures under test in a laboratory. There was little opportunity for rest.

As the flotilla neared the Azores, tension increased. Ships' wirelesses chattered of enemy submarine action in the Mediterranean and off Gibraltar. United States and British cruisers were on call to augment the two destroyers, but the larger men-of-war had thousands of square miles of ocean to patrol.

On October 9, word flashed from a destroyer through

the flotilla: *"We are entering submarine waters. Condition Two."* In response to the last two words, additional lookouts were posted—necessary but exhausting for the men because it meant longer hours on duty.

While the Azores were still a day and a half over the horizon, long waves called "ground swells" rocked the vessels. At noon, three sub chasers pulled up to the tanker for gas. The big ship slowed to eleven knots. Hawsers were strung, lashing a submarine chaser to each side of the *Chestnut Hill,* while the third chaser, *Number 219,* took position 200 feet directly to the rear. Fuel lines were passed and secured. When the sub chasers were ready, gas pumps moaned as the men began the task of pumping 2,400 gallons of gasoline into each chaser.

Chief Gunner's Mate Oscar Schmidt watched his forward gun crew go through a loading drill, and then ordered his men below for dinner. Two men remained on duty at the cannon. Young Schmidt walked aft. He was dressed in dungarees and a white sailor's cap.

Just as he reached the stern of the tanker, the submarine chaser *219* burst into flames and exploded, blowing part of the crew overboard. The *Chestnut Hill* shook and rattled as if a torpedo had been slammed into her.

Schmidt ran down a ladder to the two men at the after gun. No submarine was in sight, nor were there trails of a torpedo in the green water.

Sailors on the tanker went into action fast, seizing axes and slicing the hawsers and fuel lines leading to the three chasers. The fleet of seventy-five sub chasers scattered. In order to save his vessel, the captain of the *Chestnut Hill* signaled his engine room, "Full speed ahead!" and the tanker lunged forward.

The *219* looked like a floating volcano. Red flames speared upward through the black and blue smoke boiling from its deck. A sailor, his leg askew at an awkward angle, dangled from a line at the bow of the *219* screaming for help. No one seemed to hear him.

A sub chaser scuttled past the *Chestnut Hill* on its way to safer water. Schmidt, at the stern of the tanker, yelled as loudly as he could, "Rescue that man!" But there was no response. Although the man hanging from the bow of the tortured *219* was waving his hand, no one but Schmidt seemed to see him. The distance between the fast-departing tanker and the wrecked sub chaser was now about four hundred yards, and each second it was becoming greater.

Oscar Schmidt took a chance. Kicking off his shoes, he dived over the side and swam toward the *219*. When he was at the top of a ground swell, he could see the wrecked chaser ahead, but when he was in a trough between the waves he could see nothing.

At last Schmidt reached the bow of the burning vessel and ordered the stranded sailor to let go of the rope and jump into the water.

"Can't do it," the man replied. "My leg."

"Come on!" Schmidt ordered, and finally the man obeyed.

Schmidt kept the injured man afloat and swam with him to the stern of the *219*. There was no other place to go. Pushing the battered sailor up over the low stern, he clambered up after him.

The wrecked sub chaser proved to be an uncertain refuge. Another explosion rocked the little ship, and Schmidt waved his arms frantically, hoping someone would see him. Smoke billowed over the deck, and ammunition exploded up forward. Meanwhile the deck was getting unbearably hot. To keep the sub chaser from further damage, Schmidt unchained the four depth charges and rolled them over the side. He moved out of the smoke as best he could and waved his arms, but other vessels of the fleet were intent on placing as much distance as possible between themselves and the helpless sub chaser. They feared there would be more explosions.

The curtain of burning fuel lifted. Up forward, near the prow of the *219*, lay a man who seemed to be burning to death. The flames crackled as the little ship listed to port. Schmidt ran forward through the flames, seized the man, and hauled him to the stern.

Behind the Y-gun lay another man. This sailor was on his hands and knees, just coming to after having been knocked unconscious. Schmidt proceeded to drag this third sailor to the stern area where the others were lying.

Another explosion shook the *219*. Its list became steeper. There seemed to be no hope of another boat's coming to the rescue.

"We'll go over the side," Schmidt said to the three men. "Can you swim?"

"I am blind," said the man who had been dragged from the fire.

"Can you swim?" Schmidt demanded again.

Two of the injured men said, "Yes." The sailor who could not see did not answer.

The deck beneath Schmidt and his three charges started to burn. He helped the three men into the water and plunged in beside them. Grasping the arm

of the blind man, he swam slowly away from the sink-
ing sub chaser. After every other stroke he assisted
the man whose leg was injured.

Later Schmidt said that the most amazing thing to
him was the fact that they managed to make some
progress.

The knot of four men in the water seemed pitifully
small. Whenever they rose to the top of the ground
swells, Schmidt waved an arm, hoping to attract
attention. He battled to keep his men afloat.

Finally, some men in a dinghy from submarine
chaser *111*, who were searching the area, spotted them.
But when Schmidt and his three charges were lifted
into the tiny rowboat, it shipped water and almost
sank. To restore balance, young Schmidt dived over

the side and swam a few strokes to the stern of the
dinghy just as readily as if he had been swimming in
the Delaware River. He grasped the back of the rowboat as it slowly made its way back to the *111*.

When Oscar Schmidt was transferred back to his
tanker, a rope ladder was lowered for him. As he
reached its top, the captain of the *Chestnut Hill*
grasped his hand and said, "Schmidt, I never thought

I would see that Dutch face of yours again."

In the Azores, Schmidt had no time to visit the three men he rescued from the sea because the tanker was ordered to take on water as ballast and sail without delay to the United States. He never learned what happened to them, although later he heard a rumor that the man who had been burned had died and been buried in the Azores.

When the *Chestnut Hill* docked in the United States, Chief Schmidt was assigned the duty of drilling recruits in the Philadelphia Navy Yard. On January 25, 1919, after morning drill, instructions were given that all hands should stand by for a special formation.

Schmidt had no idea why the formation had been ordered. The column of sailors formed and Chief Schmidt marched at the rear of his recruit company, concentrating on the men's appearance and the rhythm of their step. After the ranks had formed and halted, the adjutant commanded, "Present arms!" The band played "The Star-Spangled Banner." Then the rifles were lowered, and the adjutant announced, "Chief Gunner's Mate Schmidt, front and center to receive the Medal of Honor."

It was hard for Schmidt to move. But he finally managed to leave his place behind the recruit company and march to the front of the Colors. The band broke into "Anchors Aweigh." When Schmidt halted in front of the commandant of the Philadelphia

Navy Yard, he saluted. Commodore Leeper returned Schmidt's salute, shook his hand and, after the adjutant read the citation, placed the precious Medal about Oscar Schmidt's neck.

Schmidt was discharged from the Navy in 1919 and had a hard time finding work. He was married and had a family of three to support, so he moved to York, Pennsylvania, where he went into the business of erecting bank vaults with his father. The two Schmidts were successful and accepted jobs of erecting some of the largest vaults in this country, in Mexico, and in Japan.

During World War II, their company built a new plant for the manufacture of the 40-millimeter Bofors gun for Great Britain and the United States. The gun was useful against low-flying enemy aircraft and could also be mounted on light tanks.

3

SERGEANT YORK, Tennessee Marksman

Not until the summer of 1918 did American intervention in World War I make itself felt decisively.

Although the Allies realized the United States was not prepared to fight, they became increasingly impatient for American military aid. The Allied cause hung by a thread.

On the Western Front, trenches cut up the land, extending from Nieuport, Belgium, to Switzerland. In some places they were as close as thirty yards, and in others they were separated by as much as two miles. There were rows and rows of these trenches, one behind the other. Miles of barbed wire protected them, and pillboxes, small concrete houses harboring machine guns, dotted the landscape. Trench warfare was bloody and depressing. It was an around-the-clock operation, with patrols stabbing into the night across no man's land, the area between the front-line trenches. The patrols were attempting to discover what the enemy was doing. Artillery in great masses supported straight-ahead attacks that gained but a mile or two, and in each headlong effort thousands died.

In 1918, the generals of the Allies were convinced that an all-out attack might produce a decision. As part of the plan, the United States Army, under General John J. Pershing, was given the task of attacking east of the heights of the Meuse River in September, about 125 miles east of Paris. This area had been carefully fortified by the Germans during the four years they had occupied it, so that a tangle of forest land and fortifications covered the countless hills.

In the Argonne Forest, a redheaded, rawboned corporal in the 82nd Division performed one of the most famous feats of arms in American military history. His name was Alvin C. York, and he was a soldier who, at the outset, had not wanted to fight at all. When he received the postal saying that he had been drafted, York wrote in protest to President Woodrow Wilson, saying that he was a leader in the Church of Christ in the Christian Union. Alvin York never received an answer from Mr. Wilson, so he had to choose between being classed as a draft-dodger or reporting to the Army. This was a soul-searching time for York, but he finally reported for his Army physical examination, and the doctor passed him quickly.

The next problem developed at Camp Gordon, Georgia, where the 82nd was in training. York, a huge hulk of a fellow, could lie on the firing point at the range with his 1903 Springfield rifle and send bullets cracking down the range into the bull's-eye. The distances were 200, 300, and 500 yards, and it made no difference to him whether he was firing from a standing, prone, or kneeling position.

But when York was asked to fire at silhouette targets representing men, he balked. He requested permission to see his company commander, Captain E. C. B. Danforth. "Sir, I am doing wrong," Private York said to the captain. "Practicing to kill people is against my religion."

Captain Danforth reasoned with York, giving him every argument he could think of to convince him that he should fight for his country, but York would not be budged. He was determined to leave the Army, even though it meant work at hard labor in a detention camp for conscientious objectors.

The captain asked the battalion commander, Major George E. Buxton, of Providence, Rhode Island, a student of the Bible, to talk with York, and the major argued the matter with the blue-eyed Tennessean for the better part of three days. Buxton pointed out that the great heroes and leaders of the Old Testament were staunch men who fought for their homes and people. York kept saying, "But the Old Book says, 'Thou shalt not kill.' "

Finally Major Buxton sent York back to his home on the wild Wolf River on leave and told him to think the problem through carefully.

In two weeks Alvin York was back. He looked peaceful, and said he was ready to fight.

Thirteen months later, in Argonne, York was a corporal in a platoon that had been raked by German machine guns. The platoon leader lay dead; so did the noncommissioned officers—every one, that is, except York. The remaining privates were frightened.

This was a terrible moment. Corporal York and seven privates lay flat on their stomachs in shell holes, surrounded by dead and wounded Americans. Overhead, bullets from a German machine gun whipcracked through the air. There seemed to be no help for the American platoon. But after several minutes, York located the position of the enemy machine gun. And while the gunners were searching for other targets, York saw his chance. Scrambling to his feet, he shouted, "Follow me!"

Alvin York and his little group ran forward, firing their weapons. They killed the Germans at the gun, but they had no time to confer about their next action because approximately thirty-five other machine guns opened up on them. Again York and his men threw themselves down, taking refuge in shell holes and behind logs. The roar of the machine-gun battery sounded like a gang of riveters working on steel.

When the fire slackened, York saw that the line of machine-gun nests was about fifty yards away. He called to his men. No one answered. York decided that his salvation lay in carefully firing his rifle.

The first thing he did was to squirm to a better firing position. Then, squinting through the peep sight of his rifle, he squeezed the trigger. The bolt of his .30 caliber rifle flew back and forth as if it were power operated. He shot twelve enemy gunners in succession. Suddenly, from another direction, six German soldiers charged him, one behind the other, bayonets fixed. York shot them, too. Later, his explanatory statement amused Americans everywhere. "I used an old turkey-shooting trick," he said, with his customary drawl. "It came to me that if I shot the

lead ones first, the others could hide behind their bodies like behind a log. If you shoot the hind turkey, the ones in front won't fly because they don't know the tail one's been hit."

When they saw the results of York's amazing marksmanship, 4 German officers and 128 German soldiers surrendered to him. A division inspector in the vicinity checked Alvin York's feat; shortly thereafter Captain Danforth promoted York to sergeant.

York's shooting and his solo attack captured the imagination of the Allied world and made him one of the top heroes of the First World War. Ferdinand Foch, who commanded the French, British, and American armies in France, told him, "What you did was the greatest thing accomplished by any private soldier in all the armies of Europe."

In February, 1919, the 28,000 soldiers of the 82nd

Division paraded before General Charles Summerall, himself a battlefield hero. York carried the division's flag. At the end of the ceremony, Summerall gathered the men about him in a hollow square and, with York out in front, the general thanked him for his services to the United States. Next, General Pershing, AEF commander, came to the division to add his appreciation for its effort and to thank York personally.

A few weeks later, under a lead-gray sky, the division again paraded, this time for its own commanding general, George B. Duncan. It was a bitter day, a setting reminiscent of the sacrifice of the 82nd. The division had lost over 7,000 officers and soldiers—killed, wounded, or missing in action. After the bands played the national anthem, General Duncan placed a blue ribbon about Alvin York's neck. Suspended from it was the Medal of Honor.

When Sergeant York returned to the United States with the men of his division he was met at the dock by representatives of many commercial and business enterprises. The agents were ready with all sorts of plans that would bring him ready cash, but he answered each simply, "Uncle Sam's uniform's not for sale."

Everyone wanted to see the hero. At the New York Stock Exchange he was carried about the floor on the shoulders of businessmen, and on Capitol Hill Congress gave him a standing ovation. What York did and said made front-page news; people expected he would tour the country.

But he was not interested in fame. When questioned at dinners about his amazing exploit, York would blush and answer in his soft drawl, "It was nothin'. I wanted to do the best I could." After he returned to Tennessee he talked of his prolonged questioning by reporters. "I was sorter feeling like a red fox circling when the hounds are after it. They asked me that many questions that I kinder got tired inside my head and wanted to light out and do some hiking."

Hollywood made a movie, *The Life of Sergeant York* —and trouble began. York, who received money for assisting with the picture, promptly decided to help his mountaineer friends and their children by founding the Alvin York Agricultural Institute and the York Bible Institute. However, clouds followed his happi-

ness in assisting others, because in a few years the
Internal Revenue Service claimed he owed $172,000
in taxes and interest on royalties from the movie. York
denied this, pointing out what he had done with the
money. He told his family, "I paid 'em all the tax I
owed 'em, and I don't owe 'em no more."

After ten years of litigation, the government decided
it would settle for $25,000, but to York, who was poor,
this seemed a fortune. To help him, Speaker Sam
Rayburn of the House of Representatives led a drive
to raise the money. When the last dollar had finally
been paid, York said he was "mighty grateful."

To keep busy, the big, broad-shouldered mountaineer served as superintendent of Cumberland State
Park, near Crossville, Tennessee, and in his spare time
he took to the fields and woods with friends to hunt
quail and turkey.

The old soldier's later years were clouded with
illness and worry about money. After suffering a series
of strokes and heart attacks, he had to move about in
a wheel chair. When he died in 1964, millions of
words were written about him. President Lyndon
Johnson said, "Sergeant Alvin C. York stood as a
symbol of American courage and sacrifice for almost
half a century."

The President designated General Matthew B.
Ridgway, former chief of staff of the United States
Army and a World War II leader of the 82nd Division,

as his personal representative at the funeral. In the
Wolf Run Cemetery, beside the flag-covered casket,
stood Governor Clement of Tennessee, General Ridgway, York's five sons and two daughters, and relatives.
Riflemen fired three volleys over the grave, and the
shots echoed and reëchoed through the hills that York
loved. A bugler sounded "Taps." An American
Legion Honor Guard and York's devoted friends
saluted the memory of the simple man whose name
had become, within his own lifetime, a synonym for
bravery.

4

FRANK LUKE,
The Arizona Cowboy

The airplanes of 1918 had open cockpits and simple instrument panels, and they were rickety and risky. The panels, rimmed with padded leather which aviators hoped would protect their teeth in a rough landing, contained only gas gauges, bank-and-turn indicators, and compasses. A tiny windshield afforded a little protection, but the wind screamed around it and through the wires of the struts as if warning the pilot that the fabric of the wings could tear away.

At the start of World War I, the aviators fought their own war. These "knights of the air" engaged the enemy in individual combat and flew on lonely scouting missions. As the war continued, however, it became apparent that planes could be more effective if they were employed in groups. Not every pilot liked this new idea; one who violently disliked it was Second

Lieutenant Frank Luke, Jr., a hot-tempered cowboy from Arizona.

The pilots of the 27th Aero Squadron of the American Air Service did not know what to make of Frank Luke. He was boastful to the point of arrogance, and he was not a skillful flier. But he had a record of downing fifteen German observation balloons and three enemy planes in seventeen days. Major Harold E. Hartney, the commanding officer of the squadron, knew the secret of Luke's success, for he had taken Luke aloft to shoot at toy balloons. While up there he had seen the Westerner puncture the bal-

loons as calmly and efficiently as he would have had they been anchored in a shooting gallery. Hartney understood Luke, but the other pilots had no use for him. They called him the "Arizona Boaster" and avoided him.

Luke's best friend was his wingman, Lieutenant Joseph Wehner, whose job it was to fly his plane near Luke's right wing. Wehner was not a first-rank flier, but he and Luke teamed well in the sky and on the ground. Wehner, a quiet fellow from Everett, Massachusetts, just grinned when pilots taunted him about Luke or said, "Your blond friend is a nut." Wehner believed in Frank Luke. The quiet wingman had survived several tight situations because Luke's guns had sent their German opponents down in flames.

One September day in 1918, the team of Luke and Wehner was flying over no man's land in single-seater Spads. (The top speed of the planes was 130 miles an hour.) The two aviators had been sent to fight German scout planes, but had found none. Instead they discovered two German observation balloons anchored not far behind the German trenches. Forgetting his mission, Luke wiggled his wings as a signal, and the two Americans changed direction to attack the balloons. Immediately German Fokkers on guard over the balloons left their cloud cover and dived at the Americans.

Wehner flew away from Luke's wing to attack a Fokker. Luke raced to the two balloons, heedless of the machine gunners in the baskets slung under the balloons.

Tracer bullets from Luke's machine guns sent one balloon down in flames, and then another. A Fokker pilot dived at him and missed. Luke shot the German as he sped by. Then Luke saw something from which he never recovered: Joe Wehner and his Spad were falling across the sky. The plane's trail was marked by smoke. Luke turned and flew toward Wehner, but there was nothing that could be done to help him. Black smoke poured up from the wreck.

Back at the airdrome, Frank Luke turned in his report, and for once he had nothing to say. He changed. He became both morose and angry. The pilots of the 27th tried to console him, but he acted as if he were in a different world. Major Hartney warned that continued headlong attacks against balloons were suicide, and he arranged for Captain Edward V. Rickenbacker, one of the greatest American fliers in the war, to talk to Luke. But Hartney and Rickenbacker both failed to frighten the intense Westerner.

Luke brooded. He hated the Germans—they had killed Wehner, his only friend.

Eight days later, Luke's new wingman, Lieutenant Ivan A. Roberts, was shot down, and Luke grew more sullen. He talked to no one unless he had to. The day following Roberts' death, Luke disappeared for twenty-four hours. Absence without leave in wartime is a grave offense, but Captain Grant, his immediate superior, felt sorry for him and let him off with a reprimand.

The following day, Luke climbed into his Spad and flew away from the field to hunt Germans, without receiving orders to go into combat. After shooting down a balloon, he spent the night at an airfield other than his own. When he returned to his squadron at Rembercourt, he learned that Captain Grant had grounded him.

This infuriated Luke. He waited for Major Hartney to return from a flight and, before Hartney discovered that Luke was under punishment, asked the major for permission to go on a balloon hunt.

Hartney approved but said firmly, "Be sure you do not take off until six in the evening. This will put you in the balloon area at dark, and by that time the Fokkers will have flown home to roost. Good luck."

The lieutenant went to his locker, tugged his leather helmet over his soft whitish hair, climbed into his coveralls, pulled on his leather jacket, and stalked out. Hunting up his mechanic, Luke asked him to roll out his plane.

In a few seconds, Luke and his Spad bumped down the rough runway. Major Hartney tried to stop him, for Luke was a half-hour ahead of time. But the flier pulled back on the stick and soared toward the German trenches.

He was silhouetted against the evening sky as he flew over no man's land. The Germans greeted him with rifle fire, but their bullets did not harm Luke or his Spad. His plane buzzed on toward three German observation balloons.

Luke's love for the spectacular led him to swerve back over the American lines. He penciled a message and dropped it to the men of the 42nd "Rainbow" Division:

WATCH THOSE THREE HUN BALLOONS ALONG THE MEUSE RIVER.

LUKE

German anti-aircraft fire rose to bathe his plane. The Spad rocked like a rowboat in a rough sea, but Luke was unharmed. More shells from the batteries below burst about him. Jagged holes appeared in the wings. Luke raced straight at a balloon and sent a stream of tracers into its belly. The balloon burst into flames.

Eight Fokkers protecting the balloon line dived at him. Their bullets ripped Luke's fuselage, but he escaped and in a moment dispatched a second balloon. By the time he had turned the third balloon into a huge, flaming torch, enemy fire was cutting up his Spad. The plane nosed over and fell into a spin. Eyewitnesses, including Auguste Garré, mayor of the town of Murvaux, France, said that Luke righted his ship

when he was about fifty yards from the ground and flew toward his airdrome at treetop height.

When Frank Luke flew over German support trenches, he changed his course, making a wide, sweeping turn. Swooping down over a company of German infantry marching toward its trenches, he fired a long burst from his machine guns. Six Germans fell dead; more were wounded. But the German infantry did not cease firing. Their bullets pierced Luke's plane. It began to lose altitude; it had endured all the punishment it could take.

Luke cut the gas and made a dead-stick landing in a turnip field. The Spad bounced and crashed on its side. The engine caught fire and sent up smoke, marking the spot. Luke crawled out. He was behind the German lines.

Three French citizens testified later that Luke staggered downhill toward a stream, blood pouring from a wound in his chest.

The captain of the German infantry company that Luke had attacked from the air decided the American was too brave to kill. Two squads surrounded him, and a German sergeant carrying a white flag called to Lieutenant Luke, demanding that he surrender. Luke's answer was to whip out his pistol and shoot at the flag bearer. The infantry squads fired at Luke. More blood spouted from the gaps in his chest, and Frank Luke fell dead.

During the anxious hours at Luke's airdrome there was talk that Lieutenant Luke would be court-martialed for disobedience of orders. But when the facts were in, his unusual bravery beyond the call of duty was the deciding factor. He received the Medal posthumously, the first American aviator to win it.

Luke is not forgotten. A stadium in Phoenix is named for him, and a United States Air Force Field—also in Arizona—bears his name. Frank Luke, the self-styled "Balloon Buster," was undisciplined, but no winner of the Medal was more courageous.

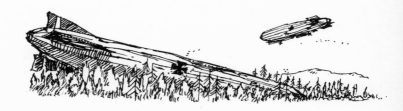

5

LIEUTENANT TALBOT
and
SERGEANT ROBINSON,
Marines of the Sky

Most of the American pilots in World War I were far better disciplined than Luke, the wild fighter from Arizona.

An aviation pioneer, Colonel William Mitchell, organized and controlled the many-sided, heterogeneous air force for General Pershing. Mitchell was eager to have his pilots used as effectively as possible and he wanted every American in the front-line trenches to recognize and appreciate the air venture. To accomplish this, he had his aviators drop informative messages to the men below. One of these read:

FROM THE AMERICAN SCRAPPERS IN THE AIR TO

THE AMERICAN SCRAPPERS ON THE GROUND

DOUGHBOYS:

While you are giving it to the Boche on the

ground, we are helping you to the limit in the air . . . Keep us posted . . . Your signals enable us to help the artillery to put their shells over your heads into the enemy.

We prevent enemy planes from telling the enemy artillery where you are; we bomb and machine-gun enemy troops whenever the chance offers . . .

Some enemy planes may break through our airplane barrage in front of you, and may sometimes bomb and machine-gun you, but in the last month we have dropped ten tons of bombs for every one the Boche has dropped. For every balloon he burns, we burn eight.

Use us to the limit . . . Burn your signal lights . . . wave a cloth . . . anything to tell us where you are and what you need.

YOUR AVIATOR

Gradually, Mitchell made the ground soldiers and General Pershing see that aviation could be helpful. But problems involving the aviators were numerous and hard to solve.

When United States Marine aviators arrived in France in August, 1918, they were eager to do their share, but they met with disappointment. There were no planes for them to fly. The pilots bore the impressive title, The First Marine Aviation Force Veterans, although they averaged less than one hundred hours in the air. To provide action for some of them, General Pershing sent three Marine squadrons to Flanders for duty with the British. It was a hazardous assignment for the Royal Air Force was losing from 52 to 97 planes a day.

One of the Marine fliers sent to Flanders was Ralph Talbot, a twenty-one-year-old from South Weymouth, Massachusetts. Ralph, or "Dick," as his friends called him, was an uncommon person.

Logan Pearsall Smith once wrote, "What a bore it is, waking up in the morning always the same person." Ralph Talbot never had this trouble; his personality and tastes were dual. He was both athletic and studious. On the one hand, Talbot loved rough outdoor ways—camping trips, football, and boxing—and sometimes when arguments needed settling quickly, he fought with his bare hands. He was also a hard-hitting catcher on the South Weymouth team, so good that he considered playing baseball for money. Because he relished vigorous exercise, he introduced cross-country running at his high school, serving as coach, captain, manager, and star runner. This sport developed his stamina, and the demands he placed on himself off the course were a vent for his leadership qualities. Talbot's competitive character sprang from his home: he was one of fifteen children.

The sensitive side of his nature was reflected in his handsome appearance. He had a shock of black hair brushed to the right, a wide forehead, and sparkling black eyes. He was president of his high-school class, a pianist, captain of the high school's debating team, a writer of promise, editor of the school's paper and yearbook, and a poet.

At Mercersburg Academy in Pennsylvania, and then at Yale University, Ralph Talbot continued to develop as a student, a writer, a poet, and an athlete. At Yale he attracted nation-wide recognition on the cross-country course and in the 1,000-yard run.

When the United States entered the First World War, Talbot told his family that he must leave Yale on completion of his freshman year. "I think I should go," he said. "I can learn to fly."

To prepare himself, he joined the Du Pont Aviation School in Delaware, and after six months enlisted in the Navy. Within two months he earned the chevrons of chief quartermaster, and in the next 120 days—time that included ground school at the Massachusetts Institute of Technology—he won his wings. Wearing the gold bar of a second lieutenant on his natty Marine uniform, Talbot arrived in France with other Marine aviators on August 1, 1918.

In Flanders, while they waited for planes to fly, the Marines were put to work improving airdromes. When a new DH-4 finally became available, the British turned it over to the Marines. Because Talbot was the top pilot of the group, it was his to take into the air.

This biplane had a top speed of 124 miles an hour and a ceiling of 19,000 feet. It was a two-seater workhorse with four machine guns—two in the nose and two in the rear cockpit. Because it had an unarmored gasoline tank between the pilot and the gunner, vulnerable even to bullets from the infantry, the DH-4 was known as the "Flying Coffin." Some called it the "Flaming Coffin."

After Talbot had taken the Flying Coffin up a few times, he reported to Lieutenant A. A. Cunningham, senior Marine aviator. Cunningham was respected. His appearance was as striking as Talbot's, and his flying background went back to 1914, when he had won his wings at Pensacola—at a time when pilots wore football helmets.

Cunningham showed Talbot the town of Staden, Belgium, on the map. It was near the coast, south of

Ostend. "Right here," Cunningham said, "is a French regiment that has been cut off by Germans. Take your plane and help the British drop food. This won't be easy," he cautioned.

Talbot was fortunate. He had requested that a first-class aerial gunner, Corporal Robert G. Robinson, a Marine aeronaut flying with the British as an observer, be assigned to him. Robinson's transfer was approved by his friend, General Mitchell. "This," Robinson wrote later, "was a happy circumstance. Talbot and I hit it off right away. I wanted to fly with the best, and that's the kind of pilot I had in Talbot."

For the next two days Talbot and Robinson flew over the German lines. The two cockpits of their DH-4 were crammed with French bread, tins of "bully beef," and other canned goods to drop on the beleaguered French regiment. The tins were packed in bags of earth to protect them from the shock of crashing into

the ground. The "bombing runs" were made at an altitude of less than 500 feet. German rifle and machine-gun bullets ripped into the wings of the Flying Coffin. Whenever the two Marines returned for gas and more supplies, mechanics crowded around the plane. They helped to restock it while the gas tanks were being filled, and made temporary repairs in the wings and fuselage. Talbot laughed. "We're just great aerial grocers," he said. "Lucky ones."

In September and October the tempo of the fighting increased. The enemy was suffering defeats on the ground, and along the 250 miles of trenches Allied soldiers were straining to end the war. A commanding figure in Flanders was King Albert I of Belgium. He had led ground attacks in person, and now he was directing the offensive to win back his beloved country.

Secret documents captured from the Germans in Flanders exposed the details of the fortified villages guarding the cities of eastern Belgium. The papers gave the locations of machine-gun emplacements, trench mortar and artillery positions, ammunition dumps, supply dumps, headquarters, and observation posts. This information was printed on special maps and handed to the pilots.

But serious obstacles awaited them. German aviators in the new D-7 designed by Anthony Fokker, a Dutch aeronautical genius in German employ, could fly faster and make tighter turns than any Allied plane in the air. German airmen were following the advice of Max Immelman, a German ace: "There's only one sure way to hit your target, and that is to fly so close that you can spit in the enemy's cockpit."

In a bombing attack against the fortified villages on October 8, the team of Talbot and Robinson again flew into action. The husky Robinson was strapped in with a belt fixed to the leading edge of the rear cockpit so he could stand up against the fierce pressure of the slip stream and man two machine guns.

Because the speed of Ralph Talbot's DH-4 was seven miles an hour faster than the British DH-9s', he was asked to fly at the end of the formation. "You can help us if we flush some Fokkers," the British pointed out.

The bombers took off, and in eighteen and a half minutes they reached a height of 12,000 feet. On the outskirts of the five-plane formation buzzed three short, chunky Sopwith "Camels"—"tricky beasts to fly," according to the British fliers. The Camel had an engine that actually rotated about a central crankshaft, and because of this it developed a torque to the right. It was hard to make a quick turn to the left in a Camel, but it could turn sharply to the right. "It can right-hand you to death," the Germans told one another.

The bombers and the Camels climbed another 2,000 feet. Although the fliers were protected from the rush of air by small windshields, goggles, leather coats, and helmets, the bitter cold made them miserable. Some wore leather face masks to prevent their noses and cheeks from freezing.

Below the Allied formation lay thick cloud cover. When gaps appeared in the clouds, the pilots could see other British planes placing smoke to help protect their advancing infantry. Suddenly black puffs of anti-aircraft fire burst about the Camels and DHs. Some of the aircraft that had been sprayed by flying bits of iron shook as if an angry monster had them in its clutches. It seemed incredible that the formation could fly on.

The lead plane swerved quickly to the right to dodge the fire. Although there was no radio communication between the planes—only from air to ground—the pilots behind the leader quickly followed suit. "Archie baiting," the British called these evasive tactics. The planes flew east for a minute, then climbed 500 feet to escape the fire of the guns.

When the lead pilot thought he was over the target, he wobbled his wings as a signal and let his bombs drop. In the foggy mist, the bombs looked like small suitcases as they arced downward. There was no way to tell if the bombs struck their targets.

Through the curtains of anti-aircraft fire, the planes sped back toward their airdromes. When the planes were ten miles inside their own lines the pilots felt safe, but suddenly, out of cloud cover below, nine

Fokker triplanes and biplanes zoomed upward. The soft gray crosses on their fuselages looked like symbols of death.

The Camels plunged into action to defend the bombers. The two formations split into dogfights. Talbot depressed the stick of his Flying Coffin and tore at the lead Fokker. In a few seconds, a triplane underneath him began firing.

Bullets cracked around Talbot and Robinson. One zipped through the overhead gasoline tank, and gas drenched the two men. It was almost impossible for them to see through their goggles; it was like looking through a rainbow. They cleaned the lenses as well as they could with the cuffs of their leather coats. The gasoline in their mouths made them choke. Four bullets tore through the plane's tail, and the stabilizer went out of action. Another bullet cut the shoulder strap on Talbot's coat.

The DH wobbled. Talbot found himself less than 200 feet from a Fokker triplane. He fired a burst; then, so Robinson's guns could fire, he made the plane skid to the right.

When Robinson bore down on his guns, the German pilot sat hunched in his seat as if trying to hide. Then the American fired another stiff volley. The Fokker turned over on its back in a lame stagger and started spinning downward, black smoke marking its path. Talbot attempted to follow the doomed airship, but two more Fokkers came at him. He ducked downward and escaped.

As the DH-4 vacillated in for a landing at the airdrome near Calais, Talbot fought the damaged controls to make a safe landing. When the two Marines dismounted, they found that a report of their action had already been filed. Lieutenant Cunningham congratulated them on their bravery, and a few hours later messages were received from British pilots thanking them.

By this time the friendship of Dick Talbot and Bob Robinson was as firm as granite. Robinson wrote of the attack by the Fokkers, "Talbot's bravery and unique flying ability saved us."

For the next few days rainy and foggy weather hindered air operations. When the rain slackened on October 13, a few Marines—Talbot and Robinson among them—flew out to bomb enemy submarine bases along the Belgian coast.

On the following day some of the Marines, in newly arrived DH-4's, were able to operate as a unit. Approximately twelve pilots manned their planes in the dull light at 5:45 A.M. The freshly painted Marine emblems looked like blotches.

The planes moaned as they took off. The fliers circled the airdrome until every pilot was up, then flew north. The targets: railway centers, railway junctions, and trains behind the enemy lines near Ghent.

Talbot and Robinson, who was now a sergeant, were again at the tail of the formation. The Marines planned to drop forty-pound bombs, return for more bombs and fuel, then continue until two thousand bombs had been placed on the targets.

On the initial outward flight, near Pittham, Belgium, twenty miles from Ghent, Talbot's plane started to cough and sputter. He levered the throttle, hoping to find an adjustment that would make the twelve-cylinder Liberty engine run smoothly. There was little else he could do. Air speed dropped. The plane lost altitude and fell behind. The DH-4 floundered like a wounded duck, rocking clumsily to the right and left.

Suddenly, out of the clouds above the formation, thirteen Fokkers roared down at Talbot's Flying Coffin. Three of the Fokkers arced back, concentrating on the disabled DH. The three Germans kept firing, following Immelman's tactic, until they were so close at times that there was danger of collision. Talbot maneuvered the Flying Coffin skillfully. When a Fokker flew at him he blasted it and swerved sharply so that Robinson could fire from the rear cockpit. The Fokker rolled over and spun downward, as if it were following the trace of a giant corkscrew.

The second Fokker roared down and sent a bullet into the DH, striking Robinson in the arm and carrying away most of his elbow. At the same time, Robinson's gun jammed. He worked to clear it with his

other hand. Talbot, looking back, saw that Robinson
was wounded but was almost ready to open fire again.
No friendly planes were around.

To escape, and to give Robinson time, Talbot
pulled back on the stick and performed an acrobatic
maneuver with the plane. The third Fokker zoomed
up, two of its bullets smashing into Robinson's stomach
and a third hitting him in the hip. Now unconscious,
Bobby Robinson slumped toward the floor, his safety
belt holding him partially in the slip stream. Ralph
Talbot, swerving to get his nose guns on the Fokker,
shot it down, then twisted around in his seat. His
friend appeared to be dying.

Talbot dipped the plane and looked for a first aid
station. He spotted a red cross behind the American
lines, just across from the German trenches. It was
hard to fly the DH-4 because Robinson had a foot
jammed against the control cables that connected the
rudder with the stick. The rents and tears in the
fuselage aided the wind in its unearthly scream
through the struts and wires.

Before he could get away, the remaining Fokker
returned and dove at the laboring DH. To evade his
enemy, Talbot hedgehopped a grove of trees, twisting
and turning. Bullets cracked upward from a German
trench as he skimmed over it at an altitude of fifty
feet. He wobbled in for a landing on rough ground
near the American first aid station, where he placed

Robinson in the hands of hospital corpsmen. The husky Marine was still alive.

Talbot's DH-4 bounced as it taxied down the field to climb back into the air. It flew just above an artillery position, then groaned upward.

At the airdrome near Calais, Ralph Talbot, now the most famous flier in his squadron, made his report. The riddled plane was mute evidence of the determination of the two Marines.

Eight days after the fight against the three Fokkers, Ralph Talbot attended funeral services for two Marines who had been shot down near the Belgian border. Three days later he was given a DH-4 to test. Shortly after the take-off, the plane's motor stopped, and the DH plunged headlong into an embankment. Instantly it became a "Flaming Coffin," and Talbot's life ended.

Two years after his death, Talbot was awarded the Medal, posthumously. His memory was honored by the naming of a destroyer the USS *Ralph Talbot*. He has not been forgotten in his home town of South

Weymouth. There a square, a street, and a memorial hall have been named in his memory. At Mercersburg Academy an oil portrait of him hangs in one of the large gathering rooms—with his Medal, lent by his mother. At Yale, his name is inscribed on a tablet in the Memorial Rotunda of Woolsey Hall, where Yale University's dead in the First World War and in other wars are honored.

The doctors' care and Robert Robinson's splendid physique enabled him to recover eventually from his severe wounds. When he was well, he received a second lieutenant's commission. By 1919, Robinson had been promoted to the rank of first lieutenant. One day while he was opening his mail he found the Medal of Honor in an envelope. "I did not know what it was," he wrote. He, too, had received his country's highest honor for his heroism in action.

Robinson finished his formal education at the University of Michigan, and when the United States entered the Second World War, he worked for the Department of Justice.

6
LOUIS VAN IERSEL,
Sergeant Extraordinary

The bulk of the fighting near the end of the First World War consisted of hard, headlong attacks by the Allies on the Western Front. The disheartened German generals conserved manpower by shortening their lines in a slow, stubborn retreat toward their homeland. In this pull-back they left tough rear guards of infantrymen, artillerymen, and machine gunners, who manned their weapons in the most strategically placed pillboxes. The idea was to make the Allied armies pay for each foot of ground.

In early November, 1918, the Allies fought desperately to force an opening in the last of the German defenses. As the Allied soldiers pushed forward, optimism arose. The slogan of the Americans, as they fought their way through the Argonne Forest and along the Meuse River, was "Out of the trenches by Christmas!"

But the Americans faced every conceivable kind of obstacle. One barrier was a wrecked bridge over the Meuse, north of Verdun, at the town of Mouzon, France. The bridge, which had been almost totally demolished by the Germans, was well guarded to prevent its repair. At this bridge, one of the most amazing soldiers in the American Expeditionary Force, a man whose reputation for fearlessness was well known in his unit, etched his name on the scroll of military history.

The soldier selected to lead a patrol through the wrecked timbers of the bridge over the Meuse was a twenty-three-year-old corporal, Louis Van Iersel, who was christened Ludovicus Maria Matheys Van Iersel. "I changed my name," he said, "because they wanted me to write it all out on the payroll."

Van Iersel, five feet three inches tall, was a spark plug in his unit, Company M, 9th Infantry. He was a hero long before he ventured into the night toward the wrecked bridge. Van Iersel was a favorite, not only because he could laugh at trouble, but because he often agreed to be the point of patrols in no man's land. Patrol leaders wanted him at the point of patrols because he could speak German. If they encountered the enemy in the darkness, they counted on him to parley with the Germans to gain time and information.

Van Iersel had been born in Holland. As a boy he

skated on the canals in winter and swam in them during the summer. His mother, however, viewed swimming as an unhealthful sport, and consequently he never became an expert in the water. While a mess boy on the Holland–American liner *Zuiderdyk,* he had an adventure 200 miles off the Orkney Islands that made him wish he were a more skillful swimmer.

The *Zuiderdyk,* en route for New York, was carrying a strange cargo: twelve thousand canary birds on its middle and upper decks, and mysterious boxes stacked on the lower deck and in the hold. The crew did not know what the boxes contained, but when a German submarine slammed torpedoes into the *Zuiderdyk* the sailors concluded that the boxes held goods considered contraband by the Germans. "They couldn't have been after the canaries," Van Iersel said later.

For ten hours, Van Iersel and others from the Holland–American ship drifted in lifeboats before being picked up. During this time, with rough water pounding at the boats, Van Iersel worried because he could barely swim.

Two years later Louis Van Iersel was standing the wheel watch at night on the Danish ship *Olaf Mearsk.* The *Mearsk* was riding a storm off Newfoundland, bound for New York. Van Iersel spotted three red lights and reported this to the captain. The *Olaf Mearsk* came about and, in the dim light, the sailors saw a small ship in distress—the 200-ton British fishing

ship *Little Secret.* Van Iersel was one of three volunteers who rowed a lifeboat 500 yards over the moun-
tainous waves. While floating alongside the *Little
Secret,* the lifeboat was almost smashed by the sea, but
Van Iersel and his companions managed to rescue the
crew. For this, each of the three volunteers received
five pounds in gold from the King of England, the
British Life Saving Medal, and the medal of the
Benevolent Life Saving Association of New York.

Each voyage to the United States made Van Iersel
yearn more and more to become an American. Finally,
in 1917, he abandoned his job as a seaman and obtained
work driving a coal cart in Passaic, New Jersey. In
the excitement of the United States' declaration of war,
Van Iersel rushed to a recruiting station, but the officer
there turned him down because he could not speak
English.

However, he found a helpful sergeant. "I mem-
orized the answers the sergeant gave me," Van Iersel
said. "This was fine, but the next day there was trouble
when drill started, because they found I could speak
only Dutch, Flemish, French, and German. No English. They took me for a German spy and put me on
kitchen police for three months so they could watch
me. A Mrs. Williams, a lady working at the Y.M.C.A.,
coached me in English, and I worked long hours. By
the time M Company reached France I could speak
English and, as I had learned a lot of things, I got the

two stripes of a corporal."

In its first test under fire, Van Iersel's unit of the 2nd Division encountered fresh German troops close to the Soissons–Château-Thierry highway.

Suddenly it seemed as if hell itself had broken loose. Gas rolled over the Americans, and they were peppered by artillery fire. The crack of the shells seemed almost as bad as their lethal striking power. Many from M Company fell. On the third day of this fierce fight, the 2nd Division was forced back slightly. Wounded men lay in front of the trench M Company had hastily dug for safety. Van Iersel and a comrade volunteered to go back into the line of fire to rescue the wounded.

Machine-gun bullets spat at the two rescuers. Carrying a man while wearing a gas mask is exhausting. Nevertheless the two men brought back seventeen wounded. On Van Iersel's eighth trip, a bullet ricocheted upward and ripped his arm like the slash of a knife. He staggered back and fell into the trench. Hospital corpsmen carried him out of the trenches on a stretcher. He was then transported across France by

ambulance and train to a hospital at Nantes. There
he was awarded the *croix de guerre,* a French military
decoration for heroism in combat.

At Nantes, Van Iersel was unhappy to learn that
when he recovered he would not be sent back to M
Company. Instead he would be assigned to another
unit—"any unit," he was told, "where they need men."

"This made me sick," Van Iersel said. "We had a
spirit in M Company like a good family. Friendship
like brothers. We had eleven nationalities in the company, and roll call sounded like a league of nations.
Captain Janda knew how to lead. So it was me for
Company M."

One night when his wound was better, Van Iersel
deserted the hospital and caught a train for Paris. He
paid his fare with money he had made by washing
and ironing shirts for soldiers before M Company had
entered the fight. He walked out of Paris and caught
a ride in a truck train headed for the front. When the
trucks reached their destination, he began walking
again. No one seemed to know the answer to the question he asked over and over, "Where is the Second
Division? Do you know where M Company is? Ninth
Infantry, American Second Division?"

But Van Iersel's facility with languages aided him.
Near Soissons he encountered French units. They fed
and sheltered him and told him the 2nd Division was
at Bulgneville, west of Chaumont. Six days after he

had left the hospital near the coast, Corporal Van Iersel reported to his company.

"Well, Dutch," a sergeant said as he grinned, "where have you been?"

A few days later, when his arm was practically healed, young Van Iersel led a reconnaissance patrol toward the German lines. It was difficult going. Deep mud, old barbed wire entangled with new barbed wire, and shell holes made the land a desolate slough. Although he was in command of the patrol, Van Iersel was again at its point so he could speak to any Germans they might encounter.

Intermittent artillery fire was churning the mud ahead, so Van Iersel placed his men in shell holes while he slipped into a trench to scout. The trench zigzagged toward the enemy main line of resistance. He turned a corner and came face to face with five German officers who were studying a map. With his pistol pointed at them, Van Iersel commanded them in German to surrender. There was a discussion. "You are surrounded!" Van Iersel shouted. "Hände hoch!"

One of the Germans blew his whistle. Van Iersel's patrol heard and ran to the top of the trench, rifles ready. At the same time, sixty German soldiers began to file out of the dugout, one by one. The Americans stood on top of the trench, their rifles aimed at the enemy, and ordered the Germans to drop their weapons.

"Place them in a pile," Van Iersel commanded. When he had his prisoners in formation and his patrol about them as guards, he marched the party back to M Company's trench.

When report of the action reached higher headquarters, another *croix de guerre* arrived for the small corporal.

It was obvious to the men in M Company that in Corporal Louis Van Iersel they had one of the great infantry heroes of the war. The question in their minds, as Van Iersel continued to lead patrols into no man's land, was *would he survive?*

The war ground on, and in November, 1918, the Allied divisions were pressing the Germans toward their homeland. But suddenly the U. S. 2nd Division ran up against an obstacle at the Meuse River. The Germans had almost wrecked the bridge at Mouzon and had fortified the other side, making it impossible for M Company to get across.

At about ten in the morning, Van Iersel received orders for his mission. There was an estimated force of about thirty-five Germans on the other side of the swift stream. Two German sentries guarded the bridge. It was Van Iersel's job to cross the river and find out what was on the other side.

At nine that night, Louis Van Iersel led a patrol of six men toward the bridge. Somewhere across the river a machine gun stuttered. Red streaks cut through the

night, but because the gun fired in short bursts it was difficult to determine its precise location. Finally, the machine gun stopped firing.

When the seven Americans arrived at the wrecked bridge, Van Iersel halted. The only noise was the swish of the current as it swirled around one of the piers. From the hill on the other side of the river a flare arched into the sky. The patrol threw itself into the mud and remained motionless. The greenish-yellow light, suspended by a tiny parachute, floated gently down to the river. In the eerie light the bridge looked like a huge pile of steel and wooden jackstraws. When the light went out, the darkness seemed blacker than ever; the village of Mouzon across the stream was but a blur.

Van Iersel placed his patrol in positions behind wrecked timbers along the bank, then tiptoed toward the bridge. Gripping his rifle in one hand and keeping his other hand close to his trench knife, he walked through the demolished structure. Another flare snapped into the sky, and two machine guns thundered at the bridge. Van Iersel lay flat as the bullets whined

and cracked against the wrecked members. When the light was out and the enemy guns were quiet, Van Iersel stood up again and inched his way ahead.

Guns of the U. S. 1st Division on the left opened up, forming a red backdrop for a blue-black hill. The roar echoed down the valley of the Meuse. A machine gun in a pillbox just across the stream, firing in bursts, barked nervously at the bridge. Its bullets whizzed over Van Iersel's head. Van Iersel hugged the wrecked floor until the machine gun stopped, then crawled on.

Suddenly a plank broke and he plunged into the river. The accident set off an alarm devised by the Germans to ring a bell on the far shore. Flares shot into the air, and German machine guns ripped tracer bullets into the bridge and sprayed the river.

The getaway man of the patrol tore from his hiding place and ran back to the headquarters of the battalion. There he reported breathlessly that bullets were hitting the bridge, that a bell was clanging, and that Van Iersel was dead.

"They can't kill Van Iersel," the clerks at headquarters answered.

In the meantime, Van Iersel was fighting for his life in the water, for the weight of his rifle was pulling him down. The current banged him against a slippery pole and a beam of the bridge that was lying awash. He managed to struggle into the wreckage. Water poured over his dish-shaped helmet, almost swamping him.

The town and the hill across the river looked alive. Van Iersel located seven machine guns, some of them firing from houses and some from trenches. Bullets whined into the twisted bridge.

When the flares died out and the guns were quiet, Van Iersel realized for the first time that the water was cold. He was about to try to swim to safety when, in the murky light, he saw a German patrol searching the water's edge. The men were about fourteen feet away. Van Iersel eased deeper into the river but maintained his grip on the slippery timbers.

He heard a German say, "I don't like that barrage. We are too close to the Americans. When it comes down tonight it could hit *us,* not the Americans. It would be a fine thing if our gunners killed three or four hundred of their own men, wouldn't it?"

Ten minutes after the patrol disappeared into the night, Van Iersel lodged his rifle in the wreckage and let go his hold. The current flung him downstream like a chip. He fought to keep his head up. Finally the water threw him against the bank, and he was able to climb out of the river.

When Van Iersel walked into the dugout that housed the battalion headquarters, the officers seized his hand. "How long were you in the river?" one asked.

"One hundred years," Van Iersel said.

From Van Iersel's exact information, his battalion commander was able to state in a report to higher headquarters that M Company would have suffered many casualties if it had tried to cross the impassable breach. A great many lives would have been lost in rushing the bridge.

Two days later, at mid-morning, on November 11, 1918, there was a silence—absolute and complete. The guns had roared for so long that their explosions seemed almost normal; this sudden silence was strange, as if a new deviltry was about to be perpetrated.

In the afternoon Van Iersel and a friend walked out on the bridge, where Van Iersel retrieved his rifle. Soon afterward he met some German soldiers and had a chance to talk to them. In telling of this later, he summed up the tragedy of war.

"They are as happy as we are," he said, "that we do not have to fight each other."

Louis Van Iersel was promoted to sergeant, and a month after his exploit at the Mouzon Bridge he stood before General Pershing, who placed about his neck the Medal of Honor.

In the Second World War, the indefatigable Van Iersel enlisted in the United States Marines and served as a technical sergeant on Bougainville Island in the southwest Pacific, during the fight against the Japanese.

PART TWO

World War II
1939-1945

7

"HANK" ELROD
at Wake Island

In 1941 World War II was raging relentlessly in Europe and Asia. Hitler's seemingly invincible German forces were advancing on every front; France had surrendered the previous year, and now England seemed ready to collapse. In Asia the Japanese were threatening Indochina and Thailand, but the United States still hoped that the issues in the Pacific could be settled peacefully. At tiny Wake Island, nevertheless, American Marines and Navy men were working feverishly to strengthen their defenses, for the little U. S. outpost was only 1,500 miles from Tokyo.

Then on a quiet Sunday morning, December 7, 1941, Japanese carrier-based planes staged a treacherous hit-and-run attack that almost wrecked the United States fleet and critically damaged its powerful base at Pearl Harbor, a few miles from Honolulu. The United

States—in a state of shock—was officially plunged into war the following day.

When word of the devastating sneak attack reached Wake Island, four Marine pilots immediately boarded their stubby Grumman F_4F_3 "Wildcats" and took off in search of the enemy. Since Wake was sure to be attacked soon and since there was no radar to give warning, the fliers were anxious to protect the garrison of approximately 500 Marines and 1,000 civilian workers.

The lead pilot was Captain Henry Talmage Elrod, a handsome, lean spike of a man from Thomasville, Georgia. The planes that he and his three companions flew were antiques, flown in from the carrier *Enterprise*. The Wildcats lacked both armor protection and self-sealing gas tanks.

Wake Island was a picture of tranquillity when Elrod and his pilots flew away from it. Far beneath them the atoll, with its crystal-blue lagoon surrounded by a white ring of foam, looked like a jewel. But its beauty had lost its appeal after Pearl Harbor. Uppermost in the pilots' minds—in the minds of all on the island—was the question: How soon would the enemy appear?

While Elrod and his scouts were north of the atoll, flying at an altitude of 12,000 feet, thirty-six twin-tailed Japanese bombers, flying from the south, glided in silently for a surprise attack at noon. A dark rain cloud hid their approach. Marine First Lieutenant W. W. Lewis, commanding a battery of 5-inch anti-aircraft guns, spotted them and spread the alarm by field telephone. His guns barked, but the enemy planes, almost on top of their targets, dropped their loads.

Immediately the peaceful atoll turned into a hell. A 25,000-gallon tank of aviation gas burst into flames along with hundreds of drums of gasoline. The runway was deluged with bombs. Tents containing aviation tools and spare parts were destroyed. But, worst of all, twenty-three Marines and ten civilians died, and the Japanese flew away practically unharmed. To complete the ill fortune, Captain Elrod, in bringing his plane back to the atoll, bounded into a hole in the runway and bent his propeller.

All night the Marines worked in a blackout, burying their dead, filling in holes in the runway, bringing more ammunition to the anti-aircraft guns, and repair-

ing Hank Elrod's propeller. Lights were carefully shielded for fear they would serve as beacons for the Japanese.

The following days were filled with dreadfully similar attacks. Jap bombers flew in from their base on the island of Roi, 720 miles to the south, and rained death on the little island. The officers in command tried to compensate for their lack of radar by having the gunners live at their guns, and by posting men on listening duty, but the constant boom of the surf masked the drone of the bombers. The hospital was filled with wounded, and at night the dead were buried in a common grave.

The incessant, fanatical bombing even made the rats frantic. One jumped into a shell hole occupied by a Marine and bit him on the nose. Since it could not be pulled off, it had to be pounded to death.

A few days after the initial attack, Captain Elrod, along with other Marines, zoomed up to fight incoming Japs. In a fearless attack on twenty-two enemy planes, he shot down two. When he climbed out of his plane, tired from the excitement and trembling like a poplar leaf, he asked Major James Devereux, of the Marines, why no reinforcements had come to help them fight. When Elrod realized there was no answer to his question, he gave orders that his plane be readied for the next day's flight.

On the fourth day a peculiar thing happened. At

three in the morning a Marine on watch reported to the senior officer, Navy Captain Winfield Scott Cunningham: "Sir, ships on the horizon." Cunningham alerted the island.

When daylight came, many believed that the ships, highlighted by the sunrise, were United States warships bent on rescue. But the Japanese gun crews soon gave notice, by firing, that the ships were not friendly. The attack was hard to understand. The Japanese were steaming in for a landing as if all the fighting men on Wake had been wiped out. The Marines figured that the enemy aviators had given false reports to their superiors.

Holding their fire until the ships were in range, the Marines then opened fire with every gun they could man. Shore batteries sank a destroyer, damaged a cruiser, and set a transport on fire. Elrod flew his single-seater Wildcat straight into the guns of the destroyer *Kisaragi,* dropped his bombs, and sank the ship. But before the vessel turned over and disappeared beneath the waves, a bullet from its deck cut Hank Elrod's fuel line.

Captain Elrod headed his wobbly Grumman for Wake with his gas dials registering zero. He barely made it, crashing into rocks on the beach. Though the Japanese landing had been temporarily thwarted, there were now only two Wildcats left to fly. When Elrod walked away from the wreck, he said to the officers and fellow pilots who had come to rescue him, "I am terribly sorry." Elrod repeated this so many times that, as grim as the situation was, his rescuers were able to smile.

Daily air strikes by Japanese bombers continued to lengthen the list of dead and wounded, but the Marines fought on with anti-aircraft guns. Life on Wake was torture. The men lived in dread of the Japanese returning and landing in greater numbers. Valiant as the Marines were, they became exhausted from work and apprehension.

When the last two planes were out of action, the Marine pilots took their places in the battle line for a last-ditch stand against the anticipated Japanese landing. The defense was now centered on a 3-inch anti-boat gun that was still operative because it was smartly camouflaged and well protected by sandbags. Captain Elrod commanded the end of the line.

At midnight on December 23, their worst fear became a reality when a fleet of Japanese warships and transports ringed the island. The hopelessness of the situation was reflected on the faces of many, but Elrod's jaw jutted out with its characteristic determination as he went about his work of checking weapons and the best positions from which to fire them. Each Marine casualty had filled him with a greater desire to make the Japanese pay as dearly as possible. He had no thoughts of surrender. He hated the Japanese.

Just before daybreak, hundreds of power launches whisked the Japanese toward shore. The Marines opened fire and sank numbers of the small boats, but the enemy pushed ashore. Desperate hand-to-hand fighting took place in the scrub magnolias not far from the water's edge. When a sergeant ran to Captain Elrod and said that his men were out of ammunition, Elrod led a counterattack so that ammunition bearers could come up. The odds against the Marines were incalculable, but Hank Elrod and others acted as if it were an even fight.

Japanese reinforcements charged up the white coral beach. The Marines were able to greet them with well-aimed fire, but more waves of Japanese landed almost intact. There was confusion; in the face-to-face fighting friends and foes were intermingled. Elrod wrestled a Japanese automatic rifle from an enemy soldier, tossed away his empty gun, and turned the Japanese weapon on the attackers. When this gun was out of ammunition, he stood up to throw a hand grenade. A bullet pierced him and he fell, mortally wounded.

Later that day Captain Cunningham faced the grim, unavoidable facts of the situation and made his lonely decision to surrender. Putting on his best blue uniform he readied himself to face the conquerors, while Major Devereux rigged a white flag as a signal. They and their men had endured fifteen days of torture. They had fought hard, but now they had no other choice than to surrender.

The survivors of Wake were treated brutally. En route by ship to a prisoner-of-war camp, five were beheaded by Japanese wielding ceremonial swords, and their bodies were mutilated by bayonets. Those who were imprisoned existed on thin soup braced by a few vegetables and horsemeat.

In a Shanghai prison camp the Marines had time to reflect on Hank Elrod. He embodied the motto of the Marines, *Semper Fidelis*—always faithful. When the Marine survivors finally reached the United States, after the Allies had at last won the war, they recommended that Captain Henry Talmage Elrod receive the Medal posthumously. At a ceremony at Marine headquarters in Washington, it was presented in Elrod's memory to his wife, Captain Elizabeth J. Elrod, of the Marine Corps Woman's Reserve.

8

"BUTCH" O'HARE,
Hero of the Navy

The Japanese, at the start of World War II, won triumph after triumph in their relentless move southward. As they advanced, leaving death and destruction in their wake, alarm spread through the Pacific to Australia.

In early 1942 the United States decided that the time had come to contain this Japanese threat. The top-ranking American leaders, General Douglas MacArthur, commander of the Southwest Pacific Area, and Admiral Ernest J. King, commander in chief of the U.S. Naval Forces, planned to strike first across the South Pacific to protect the long supply line to Australia. This was a bold and risky plan to undertake so early in the war, for it meant that carriers would have to steam 3,000 miles away from their base at Pearl Harbor into dangerous territory. Intelligence reports were clear: The enemy had two carriers and a force of cruisers, battleships, and land-based airplanes protecting the Japanese base at Rabaul, off the coast of New Guinea.

The first move in the Allied plan was to be a surprise raid against Rabaul, led by the U.S. Navy carrier *Lexington*. Aboard the "Lady Lex" was a good-looking young flier, Edward "Butch" O'Hare, who had been graduated from the United States Naval Academy less than five years earlier. O'Hare, with his easy grin and relaxed manner, was a hero to the ship's crew even before he trained the four .50-caliber machine guns of his F₄F Grumman Wildcat fighter on an enemy plane. He was the most skillful flier aboard, in the toughest branch of aeronautics—carrier flying.

The crews of the task force were briefed to the last man on the plans of Vice Admiral Wilson Brown, who flew his flag on the *Lexington*. This surprise raid was to be a joint air and surface strike.

To keep secrecy, the ships' radios were silent as the task force cut the blue Pacific on a southwest course. But when the *Lexington* and her accompanying warships were about 350 miles from the target, sailors in the radio compartment of the Lady Lex picked up a "bandit"—an unknown plane—on the radar screen. Immediately six Wildcats roared off the carrier. They shot down the Japanese scout as well as a second scout plane, but a third Japanese plane escaped and radioed the alarm.

The task force steamed on until the middle of the afternoon, when radar screens showed eighteen heavy bombers flying straight for the *Lexington*. The enemy was coming in two groups, nine bombers in each one.

The information flashed through the United States ships over loud-speakers. The sailors were already at battle stations. Captain Frederick C. Sherman, of the *Lexington,* ordered, "Pilots, man your planes!" Out of the ready room, the fliers tore for their aircraft. The deck officer signaled "Launch aircraft!" and the Grummans howled down the deck in a blur of speed.

Butch O'Hare, first off the carrier at the head of six Wildcats, maneuvered for altitude. He saw at once that he could not wait for the rest of the section because the closest group of Japanese was nearing the bomb-release point. O'Hare zoomed upward, alone. Far below, the *Lexington* was carving an erratic course through the blue water and challenging the Japanese bombers with anti-aircraft guns. Little puffs of light-brown smoke dotted the sky, but the enemy bombers flew above the anti-aircraft bursts.

The mission of O'Hare's section was *attack*. The safety of the carrier was at stake as well as the safety of every pilot who left her deck. If the fighter planes failed to stop the enemy, they were likely to have no carrier to land on. O'Hare changed his mission to an

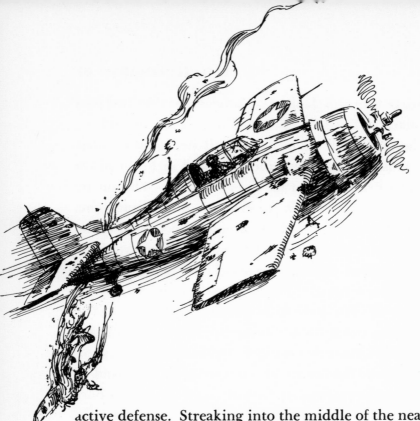

active defense. Streaking into the middle of the nearest enemy formation, the first group of Japanese bombers, he placed himself between the carrier and the oncoming group of twin-engine planes.

The Japanese gunners in the bombers blazed at him with machine-gun and cannon fire. At the same instant O'Hare, who was approximately 100 yards from the nearest enemy plane, centered his sights and shot the bomber down.

O'Hare's stubby F$_4$F looked like a speeding bumblebee as it rushed through the group of bombers. Below, on the island of the carrier, staff officers broke into a cheer and yelled encouragement for the young flier.

Admiral Brown had to remind them that they had jobs to perform. "This is not a football game," he said.

Anti-aircraft fire from the task force burst about O'Hare and the enemy planes. He continued to maneuver among them, and when he fired again he shot down four more bombers and damaged another, in less than three and one-half minutes. The Japanese planes tumbled into the sea like dead ducks. Some Japanese bombs rained about the carrier, but the huge ship was not hit.

Then O'Hare flew to help other fighters from the *Lexington* attack the second group of bombers. In this skirmish he severely damaged a Japanese bomber. But by this time the enemy had had enough; their planes turned and flew back to Rabaul.

When the battle was over and O'Hare brought his Grumman in to the 300-yard flight deck, his arrester hook snagged the cables and the plane jerked to a stop. A wild cheer went up from officers and sailors on the flight deck. Butch O'Hare, in the most daring single action in the history of carrier aviation, had saved the *Lexington*.

The projected strike at Rabaul had to be abandoned, however, because the element of surprise had been lost.

When President Franklin D. Roosevelt heard the news of O'Hare's heroism, and later reviewed and approved the recommendation for the Medal of Honor, he called O'Hare one of the greatest combat fliers of all time. Edward O'Hare went on, in other stirring, close-combat actions, to win the Distinguished Flying Cross, a Gold Star in lieu of a second DFC, and the Navy Cross. The young daredevil with the flashing grin became the idol of the Navy.

After orders transferred O'Hare, by this time a lieutenant commander, to the carrier *Enterprise,* he worked out a plan with Rear Admiral Arthur W. Radford for searching out and knocking down Japanese planes at night. The plan specified close coördination and teamwork between radar-equipped Avenger torpedo planes and "Hellcat" fighters.

One dark night in late November, 1943, near Tarawa Atoll, Japanese torpedo planes attacked the "Big E," as the *Enterprise* was often called. The Japanese dropped flares which lit up the carrier as if she were in the glare of a tremendous battery of searchlights. O'Hare, in a Hellcat, and his wingman, Lieutenant Commander John L. Phillips, in an Avenger, took off to try out the new plan. They shot down two torpedo planes in plain sight of the carrier. There was joy on the *Enterprise,* but near the end of the fight O'Hare's close friend, Captain Tom Hamilton, listening at earphones on the carrier, heard O'Hare say, "I'm shot."

Hamilton called repeatedly so that bearings might be obtained and the wounded pilot located, but Butch O'Hare never answered. For days a careful search was

made, but he was never found. O'Hare was finally
reported missing in action, but his daring flying set an
example to the Navy that has never dimmed.

A destroyer was named after Edward O'Hare, and
the city of Chicago has named an airport in his memory. At the Naval Academy, plaques bearing his picture
and his citation for the Medal are mounted in the room
he occupied as a midshipman, so that generations of
future naval officers may be inspired by his invincible
and heroic fighting spirit.

9

CAPTAIN CROMWELL,
Submariner

In late 1943, during the long, hard struggle to defeat the Japanese, the United States Fleet under Admiral C. W. Nimitz drove across the Central Pacific. Its submarines cruised far ahead of the fleet toward the Truk atoll, a powerful base for the Japanese navy, 3,200 miles from Honolulu.

The mission of the subs was to search for, report, and attack enemy ships aiding Truk and nearby islands. It was a dangerous assignment, for Japanese convoys were guarded by powerful warships equipped with the latest apparatus to send submarines to the bottom.

When the United States submarine *Sculpin* cut into Truk shipping lanes, she had an officer aboard who knew top-secret plans for the United States attack on the Gilbert Islands, and who was equally conversant with American submarine strategy and secret fleet movements. This passenger was John P. Cromwell, a tall, well-built naval officer from Henry, Illinois.

Cromwell was aboard on the *Sculpin's* scouting mission toward Truk because he would soon have to lead his wolfpack of submarines into enemy-controlled waters. On this excursion he hoped to gain first-hand knowledge of patrol routes of enemy warships and perhaps information about Japanese shipping. Danger lay in Captain Cromwell's presence aboard the *Sculpin*. If he were captured the Japanese, experts at torture, might make him expose vital top-secret information on the United States' plans and fleet movements.

The first fourteen days of the cruise of the *Sculpin* to enemy waters off Truk were routine. But at midnight on November 19, the officer of the watch notified the *Sculpin's* captain, Fred Connaway, that a Japanese freighter headed for Truk had been spotted. Captain Connaway, a quiet submariner from Arkansas, gave the information to his men over the intercom, ordered "Battle stations," and consulted his superior, Captain Cromwell.

The merchantman was well guarded by a light cruiser and five destroyers, but both officers thought that the submarine could fight and sink the Japanese freighter, or possibly a warship. Still submerged, the *Sculpin* made an emergency-speed "end run," circling far ahead of the convoy to a point at which it could lie in ambush. When daybreak came, the sub eased up her periscope. The convoy was steaming over the horizon, the Japanese men-of-war hovering about the big freighter like policemen guarding a dignitary

The huge submarine moved to a better position. The range was now 2,500 yards. The freighter looked like an easy target. Then suddenly the voice of Captain Connaway came over the intercom, warning the men at the torpedo tubes to hold their fire. "The convoy is changing its course," he said. "It is coming right at us."

Connaway himself was wondering, *Have we been spotted by the Japanese?*

The two captains conferred quickly. Although Cromwell was the senior officer and a wolfpack commander, the *Sculpin* was Connaway's vessel. Cromwell told Connaway that, as the skipper, he should make the decision. With no more hesitation, Connaway gave the order to submerge and rig for depth charges. He feared that the submarine would be bombed.

The sailors on the *Sculpin* froze in place while the convoy steamed over them. No depth charges were dropped. After thirty minutes, the sub came up; it made another "end run" and lay in wait again for the Japanese freighter.

Three hours later, when the periscope of the *Sculpin* went up—slowly—the officer at the telescoping eyepiece sounded the emergency-dive alarm. Captain Connaway shouted over the intercom, "Dive! Dive! Dive!"

Up above, the destroyer *Yokohama* cut through the waves straight at the submarine. For five hours, it hovered over the sub, dropping 600-pound depth charges.

The plates of the *Sculpin* rattled with each "ash can," as if they were about to burst. Her lights flickered out, and dim emergency lights went on. The hull cracked in the after-engine room, and water poured in. Exhaust valves, pressure gauges, and the steering gear were damaged. The temperature skyrocketed to more than one hundred degrees. Breathing became increasingly difficult because of the shortage of oxygen. But as Captain John Cromwell walked through the underwater ship, his calm manner gave the men assurance.

George E. Brown, young naval lieutenant from Cincinnati, Ohio, wrote later, "Sound detectors now reported a rain squall. This was like a message from heaven." Brown and his shipmates hoped that the *Sculpin* could escape during the storm.

The *Sculpin* ran submerged for twenty-five minutes, on a course designed to place the squall between her enemies and the spot at which she would come up. Finally, men at the sound apparatus were sure that the submarine had shaken its enemies. Pumps were started to trim the sub. Exhausted sailors formed a bucket brigade to help the pumps move the water to a different compartment of the ship. Lights grew dimmer. It was harder to breathe. Then the temporary diving officer made a bad mistake. He turned the wrong set of valves and the *Sculpin* broached her long, black nose through the waves instead of just poking her periscope up.

Captain Connaway ordered, "Battle stations," and the sub prepared to fight. Later, Lieutenant Brown wrote, "The day was a pretty one, with white caps washing the decks. At first we did not see the destroyer. Then one of the men spotted it against the sun, about 3,000 yards off, coming like the wind."

A salvo from the destroyer's guns crashed into the submarine. Sailors coming up on the sub's deck for fresh air were killed as they stepped through the hatches. One of the first to fall was Captain Fred Connaway. Fireman First Class A. B. Guillot, of New Orleans, manned the sub's .50-caliber machine gun. But when a Jap shell crashed into it, Guillot fell over the side, blood streaming from great wounds in his chest.

Lieutenant Brown, now in command of the submarine, ran below to the wolfpack commander, Captain Cromwell. Brown told John Cromwell that, much as he hated to make the decision, the *Sculpin* must be scuttled—sent to the bottom—to prevent the Japanese from capturing an ultra-modern type of United States submarine. The men, Brown said, must take their chances in the water.

Cromwell answered calmly, "Go ahead, Brown. Because I know so much about our future plans I can't go over the side with you. I'd face torture, and I might reveal information that would harm shipmates all over the Pacific. I'm going down with the ship."

George Brown saluted with awe. He ran back to the control room, rang for emergency speed, and passed the word to abandon ship.

To make sure that every man aboard knew the *Sculpin* was headed for the bottom, Lieutenant Brown sent one chief petty officer forward and another aft to spread the news. He was afraid to rely on the public address system. When the chiefs returned, one said, "Captain Cromwell is not coming. Ensign Fiedler and Apostol are playing cards in the ward room. They say they'd rather die than be captured."

Water was already waist deep in the conning tower. George Brown waited one minute, with his watch in

his hand, to give everyone a chance to abandon ship; then he turned the valves that spelled doom for the submarine.

Lieutenant Brown, who became the only surviving officer, dove over the side with most of the crew. The survivors were picked up by the *Yokohama*, where they stood by grimly on the deck, and began the lonely, miserable existence of prisoners of war.

The *Sculpin* plunged beneath the waves, carrying with her the two men who did not choose to try to escape and the brave captain, John P. Cromwell, who chose to die rather than run the risk of betraying "shipmates all over the Pacific."

The *Sculpin's* captured crew members were treated horribly on board ship and in Japan. After the war, when they were returned to the United States, they had the satisfaction of learning that Mrs. Cromwell, of Palo Alto, California, had received the posthumous award of the Purple Heart and the Medal of Honor for her husband. The men of the Navy who knew Cromwell were glad when his son, John P. Cromwell, Jr., graduated from the United States Naval Academy in 1951.

10

FATHER O'CALLAHAN
of the Franklin

By 1945, the war in the Pacific was progressing favorably for the United States and Great Britain, but an important mission still lay ahead. Before the Allies could sweep Japan's navy from the Pacific, they had to demolish or capture the heavily fortified Ryukyu Islands, south of Japan. One of the islands, Okinawa, was a Gibraltar in strength.

On March 18, the United States' aerial tactician, Vice-Admiral Marc Mitscher, sent his Fast Carrier Task Force 58 to bomb airfields in southern Japan. His object was to prevent Japanese planes from attacking the invaders at Okinawa. But Admiral Mitscher's aviators found few planes on the airfields, because the Japanese fliers had already taken off to attack the American carriers. Consequently, the Americans bombed hangars and barracks.

The next day American planes flew farther north, damaging sixteen ships of the Japanese navy. But at the same time, Japanese pilots placed two United States carriers under attack. One of these carriers was the *Franklin*—"Big Ben," her crew called her.

Of particular worry to the American sailors were the Japanese Kamikaze planes, flown by suicide-bent pilots who were determined to crash onto the deck of an enemy vessel. The pilots of these "personally directed bombs" expected to be rewarded in the hereafter for their sacrifice for the Emperor.

At breakfast time, planes leaving the *Franklin* overloaded the radarscope, and an incoming Japanese plane was not discovered. It was not a Kamikaze, but a bomber flown by a determined, fearless Japanese pilot. He dropped his bombs right in the middle of the *Franklin's* flight deck.

Instantly there was chaos. Planes on the flight deck, full of high octane gas, burst into flames as if ignited by ghostly hands. "Tiny Tim" rockets stacked on the flight deck exploded and screeched by the ship's island in a horrible display that looked like an insane Fourth of July. These powerful new weapons were capable of penetrating the toughest armor. On the enclosed hangar deck below, planes that were tuning up caught fire. Iron fragments from explosions sprayed each deck of the ship. The ship's steering apparatus went out of

action, and the *Franklin* began to drift toward Japan.

Black smoke filled the decks and corridors of the ship. Men broke out of mess lines and groped their way to the ladders that led to the flight deck. Ammunition stored in the ship's lockers or stacked at antiaircraft guns shot out in all directions. The explosions, the sheets of flame, and the clouds of smoke turned the carrier into a spouting volcano. From all directions came eerie overtones to the chaotic scene: the piteous cries of the wounded.

The new chaplain aboard the *Franklin* was wounded. A piece of flying iron cut him in the leg. But the chaplain, Lieutenant Commander Joseph Timothy O'Callahan, a Jesuit priest from Boston, did not consider it

serious. He rushed from his battle station in the carrier's island, across the slanting flight deck, to administer the last rites to some sailors who were dying. He
and his friend, Chaplain Grimes Gatlin, comforted
dying and wounded Catholics, Jews, and Protestants
alike.

Father O'Callahan seemed to be everywhere. When
red-hot 2,000-pound bombs began to roll about the
flight deck, he called for volunteers and organized them
into groups. Working together, they lifted the huge
bombs and dumped them into the ocean. Numbers
of sailors violated the tradition of the sea by abandon-
ing ship on their own, jumping over the side.

Someone told O'Callahan that there were men
trapped below decks. O'Callahan shouted for volunteers and led about a hundred men down a ladder, on
the port side aft, into one of the huge smoke-filled
rooms.

The tremendous after elevator, used to carry planes
to the desired deck, exploded with a terrific crash,

shaking the ship and making its list to starboard steeper. A smaller explosion hit some of O'Callahan's group, and a piece of steel cut the priest again in the leg. His two wounds caused his shoe to fill with blood, but in comparison with others Father O'Callahan was not severely hurt. He and his rescue force groped through the smoke toward the stern and carried badly wounded men up the ladders to the flight deck.

Commander Fred M. Reeder, on the bridge of the United States Carrier *Bataan,* not far from the burning ship, later wrote, "I saw the Japanese pilot just as he pulled out of his dive low over the *Franklin*. She was awful to look at. The bomb hit her flight deck, which was loaded with planes carrying full tanks of gas. Some planes were taking off. Tremendous clouds of smoke boiled up. The *Franklin* sheered out of formation. I told our captain I thought she was going to sink. The task force continued to launch planes as the *Franklin* fell several miles to the rear. Cruisers and destroyers formed around her and picked up men who had gone over the side."

On the disabled carrier, Captain Leslie H. Gehres gave the order to flood the magazines to prevent tons of ammunition below from exploding and sealing the fate of the *Franklin*. He was determined not to abandon ship.

Again the Jesuit leader, O'Callahan, called for volunteers and led them to the 5-inch shell magazine.

Here he and his men grabbed a hose and wet
down stacks of shells. Meanwhile, Gunners Thomas
Stoops and Arlo Catt, in charge of ammunition, turned
on emergency valves more powerful than fire hoses,
and flooded the magazine.

This mission accomplished, O'Callahan led his men
back through the hangar deck. The huge enclosed
area, as big as three football fields, was a mass of flame.
The stench of the burning dead was nauseating, and a
pall of black smoke hung down from the ceiling.

Back on the flight deck, Father O'Callahan and his
men grabbed a hose and cooled red-hot magnesium
bombs. As soon as that peril subsided, he again
traveled up and down the deck ministering to the

dying and the wounded. The priest did not seem to realize that he himself was bleeding profusely.

It was hard for other ships of Task Force 58 to help the *Franklin,* for by this time they were fighting off Japanese Kamikaze planes trying to crash on their decks. Commander Reeder wrote, "One of these suicide pilots flew at our ship. He came so close that, if he had been a friend, you could have easily recognized him. He dropped a bomb, and it hit our water line but failed to explode. Our Task Force's anti-aircraft fire was terrific. One of my friends, our group commander, Walter Etheredge, of Meridian, Mississippi, was killed by this fire. I saw his plane explode in a cloud of black smoke."

To help the badly crippled *Franklin,* Rear Admiral R. E. Davison ordered the cruisers *Pittsburgh* and *Santa Fe* to attend her. Destroyers formed a closer screen about Big Ben and continued to pick up crewmen who were in the water. The two cruisers passed towlines to the burning ship and halted her drift toward Japan.

Seven hundred and twenty-four men lay dead or wounded aboard the *Franklin;* 265 had been hurt in accidents. Had the officers and the crew not been skillful, and had they not been well trained and disciplined, many more fliers and seamen would have died.

Finally her mechanics and technicians got up steam again, and the *Franklin* limped back to Pearl Harbor for repairs. Then she traveled across the Pacific, through the Panama Canal, to New York City, where she was thoroughly overhauled.

Japanese Kamikaze planes and bombs damaged the carriers *Wasp, Bataan, Enterprise, Intrepid,* and *Yorktown,* but no carrier was harmed as seriously as the *Franklin.*

In every war, in every action of any size, men perform brave deeds that are not acknowledged. Circumstances prevent such heroes from being recognized and receiving medals. But on the *Franklin,* the selfless, brave work of Lieutenant Commander Joseph Timothy O'Callahan stood out. Men everywhere on the stricken carrier recognized his deeds as above and beyond the call of duty, and he was awarded his nation's highest military medal.

Eventually Father O'Callahan returned to Massachusetts, where he served at the College of the Holy Cross at Worcester. However, for the last seven years of his life he endured suffering brought on in great measure by his ordeal on the United States Carrier *Franklin*—an ordeal during which he had done everything in his power to save his fellow men.

11

BOB BUSH,
Fighting Medical Corpsman

Less than a month after the display of courage on the *Franklin,* a show-down fight took place for the possession of Okinawa. This last outpost for the Japanese was located only 350 miles from their homeland.

Okinawa is a rugged and strangely beautiful island. Part of its 70-mile length is covered with forests, and much of the land is sliced by ravines and ridges. Towering cumulus clouds and mists crown Okinawa part of the year; drenching rains bathe it during other seasons. In times of peace it resembles a dream island, but in 1945, seventy-five thousand Japanese had labored to make it a death trap for Americans.

They had honeycombed the ridges with tunnels so they could move safely from one concealed gun position to another. They had fortified caves and had constructed concrete pillboxes. Artillery, automatic weapons, and mortars were ready to rain death upon any attackers. In desperation, the Japanese had also decided to launch massive attacks by suicide planes and suicide boats. The latter were small craft loaded with torpedoes. They rammed deliberately into enemy vessels, hoping their torpedoes would explode and send the enemy craft to the bottom of the sea.

In spite of almost 2,000 Kamikaze attacks, and other numerous sorties against the fleet, the United States armed forces worked together to place two Army and two Marine divisions ashore on Okinawa.

A month of ghastly fighting crawled by. It seemed to the Americans that their enemies were always on a higher ridge, shooting down on them. The Japanese positions were incredibly strong—certainly among the strongest encountered by the Allies in the Pacific during the Second World War. Gains by the attackers were small, and were paid for in blood. Army and Navy surgeons worked overtime to save the men whose bodies were ripped and bruised by the bullets and shells.

To assist the surgeons, Navy medical corpsmen, who had been trained carefully back in the United States, were attached to each Marine company. The job of the corpsmen in action was to stay with the company and administer to the wounded. They were not expected to fight because, under the terms of the Geneva Convention of 1864, first-aid men were declared neutral. The Red Cross arm bands they wore around the biceps of their left arms were emblems showing that they were noncombatants entitled to safe conduct in battle.

But in 1942, when General MacArthur's men set out to stop the Japanese advance, they quickly discovered that Japanese soldiers did not know what the Red Cross brassard meant, or if they knew they did not abide by

its meaning. The Japanese in New Guinea fired on corpsmen and doctors who were taking care of the wounded. As a result, many of the first-aid men and doctors began to arm themselves with pistols. One of the Navy corpsmen on Okinawa who carried a pistol on his web belt while caring for the wounded was a rangy six-footer from the state of Washington, Robert Eugene Bush.

Bush had enlisted in the United States Navy when he was eighteen. He had been a popular high-school athlete at Willapa Valley High School in Menlo, Washington; and the men of the 5th Marine Regiment soon grew to admire him because of his fearlessness. No battle was too nerve-racking to keep young Bush away from his Marines.

This was proved in the devastating battle near Awacha, Okinawa, on May 2, 1945. On that day, pour-

ing rain and heavy clouds swept the ridges, which seemed to harbor countless Japanese artillerymen and infantrymen. It was difficult for the Marines to fire accurately at their unseen enemies, though the tanks managed to crawl forward and spray some of the Japanese caves and concrete pillboxes with napalm— jellied gasoline. The Marines who advanced on foot, however, seemed to offer easy targets for the invisible

Japanese. Machine-gun bullets and artillery shells cracked menacingly through the clouds, and Marines fell to the ground with no one being sure of the source of the bullets.

Bush and other Navy corpsmen scrambled out of their foxholes and braved enemy fire to treat the wounded in this fearful, disheartening scene.

Lieutenant Colonel William E. Benedict ordered two companies of his Marines to advance. Immediately, from the fog, they were greeted with hand grenades and knee mortars. There was no further question of the Japanese being near at hand, for these were close-support weapons. So many Marines fell that the entire battalion was in danger. Colonel Benedict called back to the Marine artillery and requested that smoke shells be fired in front of his first two companies.

When the smoke shells howled down on the little plateau, covering it, the Marines had a momentary respite, for the Japanese were thrown temporarily off balance. Marine noncommissioned and commissioned officers moved rapidly to regroup units and appoint new leaders to replace those killed and wounded.

But the letup was brief; the Japanese artillery soon lashed out again at the Americans. The Japanese had held the island for such a long time that they had range-finding data marked on their maps. Their artillery-men, though located far to the rear, could fire accurately without having to worry about fog or smoke or the necessity of posting observers up front.

Rain continued to drench the fighters. Navy Corpsman Bush, glancing up, saw Lieutenant John Francis Roach, a Marine platoon leader, on the skyline. At that instant, an enemy artillery shell burst over Roach's head. The young officer, silhouetted against the light-gray clouds, threw his carbine into the air and fell forward. Bush, carrying a bottle of blood plasma, rushed to his side.

Though blood plasma was ordinarily given by a doctor or a nurse, Bush and other Navy corpsmen had been trained to administer the life-giving fluid at moments like this.

He bandaged Roach's wounds and lashed on a tourniquet to stop the gushing blood. Inserting the blood plasma needle into a vein in Roach's arm, he straightened the rubber tube at the bottom of the bottle and held it over his head. Roach, who looked like a dead man, stirred, and Bush knew that his patient was alive.

Just when Lieutenant Roach seemed to be making strides toward recovery, a platoon of Japanese who had crept from their position on the next ridge and climbed up through a tangled ravine, jumped to their feet and charged. Bush whipped out his pistol. Holding the bottle of blood plasma high with one hand, he fired the pistol with the other. When his weapon was empty, he dropped it and seized Roach's carbine. Setting the change lever at automatic, he sprayed the enemy. Six Japanese fell, almost at his feet. A Japanese soldier shooting from the side took careful aim. His bullet struck Bush in the face and carved out his right eye.

Gunnery Sergeant Harry Davis and Corporal Edwin Fortier, who had machine guns not far away, turned their weapons on the enemy and helped stop the charge.

Two Navy corpsmen, carrying a stretcher, rushed through artillery fire to carry their comrade back. Although he was in great pain, Bush pointed to Roach and said, "Take him." Then Bush assisted three other Marines who were wounded. He staggered back through the pouring rain to the first-aid station, where he calmly disregarded his critical condition. He insisted that the surgeons care for those who might fight again and for those who were dying. No surgeon could treat Bob Bush until he collapsed.

The Marines on the embattled plateau, who had witnessed the drama on the skyline, fought harder throughout the day and into the night in violent hand-to-hand actions. Bush, the Navy corpsman, had inspired them.

Bush was taken aboard a hospital ship and then to Pearl Harbor, Hawaii, where he entered a general hospital. He suffered for a long time, but finally regained his health. As a civilian, this brave recipient of a Medal of Honor settled with his wife and four children at Elma, Washington, where he became president of a lumber company.

12

AUDIE MURPHY
of Texas

Since the middle of 1943, Americans had been fighting in Europe as well as in the Pacific. And in August of 1944 the Seventh United States Army stormed ashore in southern France with the objective of capturing the French ports of Toulon and Marseilles. Then it was to press northward and join the Allied forces that had landed on the Normandy coast and were fighting their way toward Paris.

The Germans in southern France retreated fast at first, but the Americans and their French allies discovered that the farther they went, the slower their progress and the harder the fighting. In this struggle, the Seventh Army was aided by Second Lieutenant Audie L. Murphy, well known in the 3rd Infantry Division, as well as in his regiment, the 15th Infantry. Murphy, who had reported as a private in Africa, had fought in

Sicily and earned battlefield promotions from corporal to sergeant to second lieutenant. He had been wounded twice since landing in France and had won the Silver Star twice in a span of three days, entitling him to wear the Star and Cluster.

Murphy had first met with trouble in October of 1944 while leading his platoon through a forest area of the Vosges mountain range in Alsace. The platoon's progress was good until a German sniper fired from a camouflaged foxhole at a distance of thirty-five yards. Murphy was downed by a bullet through his hip, but while he lay on the ground he killed the sniper with a single shot from his carbine. As a youth he had perfected his aim while hunting game to help feed his family.

Worse trouble came his way when he was released from the hospital. The men from his unit were engaged in one of the toughest assignments of the entire war: the reduction of the Colmar Pocket.

This "pocket" was actually a huge bulge in the American lines, with its center thirty miles from the northeast corner of Switzerland. Because it amounted to a bridgehead from which the Germans could attack in almost any direction, it was a threat to the entire Seventh Army. Word from the Underground, substantiated by photos taken by Allied aviators, indicated that increasing numbers of Germans were filling the

Colmar Pocket. It definitely had to be eliminated.

The weather at the end of January was bitter cold, with the thermometer hovering at fourteen degrees above zero. The frozen ground itself was a hazard, even though it was covered with snow, because it formed a hard surface over which German tanks could travel with ease. Since it was only a question of time before the enemy struck, the Americans decided to strike first.

Lieutenant Murphy's platoon entered the battle on the second day of fighting (January 24, 1945), advanced 600 yards, then halted until more ammunition could be brought up. On the following day Murphy was wounded again when a mortar shell exploded near him and peppered his leg with steel fragments. His friends were falling all around him, but since the company was moving on, he refused to stop for medical treatment.

His outfit, Company B, had entered the battle in the forest of the Colmar Pocket with 6 officers and 155 men. After twenty-four hours of action all that remained

were Lieutenant Murphy, another officer, and twenty-eight men. When the other officer was wounded during the night, Murphy received a message that promoted him to company commander. Just two years after joining Company B as a private, he found himself in the position of being its captain.

The night of January 25, 1945, was unbelievably cold. The firs, their branches laden with snow, seemed like inhospitable sentinels as the men plodded on to the edge of the wood. When Murphy stopped the company, he forbade the men to build fires because of the nearness of the enemy. Instead, he ordered them to stamp about in the snow to keep their feet from freezing.

When a gray-green dawn filtered through the firs, Murphy and his infantrymen saw a white field to their front with two long fingers of forest stretching toward the German-held village of Holtzwihr, about a mile away. The edge of the forest formed a big U, and Murphy's company was standing at the base of the U. He and his men looked for friendly troops but saw

none. They were isolated. Murphy worried about this and about the ground; it was frozen too hard for them to dig foxholes for shelter. The situation looked dismal.

But soon two American tank destroyers rumbled up and took position 40 yards away. Each of these 20-ton monsters had a snoutlike 75-millimeter cannon mounted in front and a powerful .50-caliber machine gun dominating its turret. No one knew how many tanks the Germans had just across the snow-covered field, but the look of the two friendly tank destroyers was heartening.

Next, a wire detail lugged a telephone line through the woods and placed a field telephone where Murphy could use it. "You can call the battalion commander on this," the wire chief said before he left. "Good luck."

Murphy waited for the attack signal, which was delayed. Suddenly, at about two o'clock in the afternoon, six German tanks, protected by about 250 infantrymen, left Holtzwihr and headed straight for Murphy's little company.

The tanks belched fire as they rolled along. Branches from trees above Company B crashed down under the withering fire. German infantrymen, marching behind the tanks, looked like ghosts because of the snow-white capes they wore as camouflage.

The two tank destroyers bellowed at the six German

tanks, but the German formation came on. The noise sounded like claps of thunder in a valley.

One of the American tank destroyers, trying to maneuver, slipped into a ditch, its guns pointing helplessly at the sky. Its tracks whirred and kicked up showers of turf and snow. The engine labored and groaned, but could not lift the bulky shell of the tank from the ditch. Its crew clambered out of the hatch and ran back into the forest. In a moment, German 88-millimeter shells crashed into the other tank destroyer, and black smoke boiled out of it. Part of its crew scrambled out and also ran for the forest.

Audie Murphy, shouting and waving his carbine, ordered his men back to a trench a half-mile away in the forest. A few heard and departed; then the rest left. Murphy was alone. When asked later why he did this, Murphy drawled, "I saw no reason for any more men to be killed when one man could do the job."

On came the German formation, belching fire, right at Murphy. It was one man against six monsters and a battalion.

Murphy grabbed the field telephone, twisted its crank to generate electricity, and yelled to a sergeant at battalion headquarters that he needed protective artillery fire. He juggled a map on his knee to answer questions about the German attack.

In a few minutes, American artillery fire came whistling down and crashed into the field. German shells added to the racket. Murphy lay down and fired his carbine at the oncoming infantry. A tree near by crashed to the ground as if it had been felled by an invisible ax. He heard a tinkle in the phone and answered it. A voice said, "How close are the Germans now?"

Murphy's answer was one of the classic statements of the war. "Just a minute," he shouted, "and I'll let you speak to one."

Murphy said later that he had no idea at the time of how he was to free himself from his predicament, and for some reason he did not care.

When his carbine was exhausted, he got one of the most audacious thoughts of his audacious career. He cast aside his gun, grabbed the telephone and all the wire he could lug, and ran for the tank destroyer. The black smoke from the burning vehicle almost choked him as he climbed to its top. He rolled the body of the dead tank-destroyer commander off into the snow, and lay down behind the .50-caliber machine gun. Threading a belt of the powerful bullets into its breech, he yanked the operating handle to the rear twice, and fired into the nearest German infantrymen.

Every few moments he ceased firing to call into the telephone for artillery fire, directing it closer and closer to his position. This was almost suicide.

German 88-millimeter shells thudded into "Murphy's fort" and shook it as a hound shakes a rabbit. Though the smoke boiling up from the open hatch helped by concealing him, it also hindered his aim.

From the edge of the forest an American artillery observer, who was unable to contact his guns because his radio was not working, saw Audie Murphy. The artilleryman wrote later, "Murphy's deed on the flaming tank destroyer was the bravest thing I ever saw in combat."

Over the telephone wire came a whisper, "Are

you still alive, Lieutenant Murphy?" Murphy quipped, "Momentarily, Sergeant, and what are *your* postwar plans?"

Through the smoke, Murphy caught sight of a column of twelve Germans near the tank destroyer, concealed in a ditch, rifles clutched in their hands. He swung the gun and riddled them.

More artillery thundered about him. Planes from the First Tactical Air Force flew over the clearing and strafed the Germans. Then Murphy's phone went dead. But just when it looked as if the Germans might take him, the German tank commanders, apparently discouraged by the loss of so many of their protecting infantry, turned about and headed for the village. Murphy was exhausted. He slid off the tank destroyer and limped away just as it blew up.

Back in the forest with his men, he led them to the clearing and placed them in positions from which they could defend if the enemy returned.

Murphy's fight stopped a German attack and enabled his division to advance. A few days later, on February third, the Colmar Pocket was reduced. Murphy's heroism was investigated, and sworn testimony was taken from men who saw parts of his deed. The story was pieced together and verified. Murphy, reading it later, said it sounded like an account of somebody else's action.

Word spread that Lieutenant Audie Murphy was

being recommended for the Medal of Honor. His officers, fearing that he might be killed before receiving the Medal, gave him a job at regimental headquarters in the rear. While there he heard that Company B had bogged down in the Zweibrücken–Kaiserslautern area. This upset him. He went to a sergeant and asked him to drive him as close to Company B as it was safe for a jeep to go. Dismounting from the vehicle, he discovered the men cowering in a trench. He coaxed them from it, reassured them and the new lieutenant who was in command, and returned to the rear.

Murphy's action at the Colmar Pocket, which won him the Medal, was that of a man with his back to the wall. It was a long shot against incredible odds. It was the fight of a man who was determined to save as much of Company B as he could.

The mild-appearing Audie Murphy became one of the best-known heroes of the war. He wrote a book about his experiences, entitled *To Hell and Back,* and a full-length portrait of him was hung in the state capitol at Austin, Texas, his home state. Wherever he went he attracted a crowd, but he soon tired of this hero worship.

James and Bill Cagney brought Murphy to Hollywood and put him under contract, with the idea of making him a star, but he never was used in one of their productions. He did get into movies, however, and in his first film, *Beyond Glory*, he played a small part as a West Point cadet. He was paid $500 and was given four shirts. He said the shirts were nearly as bad as the picture, but the film earned him another bit part.

Probably the thing that pleased him the most, after his return from Europe, was a present the people of Farmersville, his home town in Texas, gave him as an expression of gratitude. It was a check for $1,750. He and his eight brothers and sisters had grown up under great adversity, and he used the check as a down payment on a house for his sister Corrine, on condition that she and her husband take the three youngest Murphy children from the orphanage in which they had to be placed before the war.

Audie Murphy lives in Hollywood, still acts in the movies, and is a television personality.

Thousands of Americans appreciate what he did for our country, but those who appreciated him the most were the hard-pressed men of Company B.

13

BOBBIE BROWN
at Crucifix Hill

Captain Bobbie E. Brown, like Audie Murphy, won
the Medal of Honor in Europe during World War II.
A soft-voiced, husky man from Columbus, Georgia, he
was a sergeant in the Army before the war. Soon after
the United States joined the global conflict, Brown
established his potential as a brave soldier and a leader
by winning a battlefield commission in Africa.

On October 8, 1944, near Aachen, Germany, Captain Brown was in a situation that looked like an utter
stalemate. He had been given the mission of leading
his company of First Division soldiers and a platoon
of Rangers in the capture of Crucifix Hill. Tucked
into the side of the hill were approximately thirty
concrete pillboxes, sturdy forts, each about 40 by 30
feet in circumference and about 20 feet high. The

armament in the concrete forts varied. Some had 88-millimeter cannons; some mounted heavy machine guns; some had both. The surface of the hill was criss-crossed with barbed wire.

Crucifix Hill was a strongpoint in Germany's Siegfried Line. The cross on the crest, its gaunt arms stretched against an October sky, seemed to warn Brown and his men to come no closer. Enemy fire from the hill approximately 900 yards away supported this warning.

Brown studied the hill through his field glasses, then used a portable radio to call battalion headquarters to ask for help from the air. Shortly afterward B-24's of the First United States Air Force thundered over the hill and bombed it. The earth trembled; columns of dirt shot into the air. When the planes

had gone Brown saw that, although not a pillbox had been wrecked, mounds of dirt stood in front of many of them. This meant that numbers of the German guns could not fire.

Brown led his men to within 100 yards of the hill, but the firing grew so intense that it looked like certain death for anyone to approach closer.

He placed his company in the best shelter he could find and inched up the slope. It seemed to him that if three of the pillboxes on the brow of the hill could be destroyed, his company had a chance to take the hill.

Brown saw that the hill could be captured in two ways: with the help of reinforcements (but this would require time and lives) ; or by sending someone forward to dynamite the three key pillboxes. It looked too dangerous to him to order a man to crawl up the slope with dynamite, or even to ask for a volunteer. Though it was not his duty as a company commander to fight in advance of his company, Captain Brown decided to attack the pillboxes single-handedly.

He secured an armload of dynamite that was wrapped into a bundle lashed to a pole, and equipped with a fuse. With this, he crawled toward the first pillbox.

Mortar fire burst over his head, and machine-gun bullets kicked up dirt in his face. He crawled on, cradling the dynamite in his arms. When he reached the first pillbox he stood near a port, poked the satchel

charge inside, and pulled the fuse. The pillbox exploded with a roar, the concussion throwing him to the earth. Chunks of concrete rained about him.

Brown crawled back and forth two more times for additional satchel charges so he could wreck all three of the dominating concrete forts. While he stood beside the third pillbox, ready to insert his dynamite, mortar fire from the rear of the hill struck him in the knee and knocked him down. He struggled back up in spite of the pain and blood and blew up the pillbox.

Brown realized that his men could now come up on the hill and could probably capture it.

When he was back with his fighters, a medic tried to help by treating his wound, but Brown said, "We can't slow up now. If we're going to win, we have to hit the trail up there fast and get the rest of those pillboxes. It won't be long till the hill is going to swarm with Germans."

But vital questions remained unanswered. What was the best route for the company? Should it go over Crucifix Hill or around it? And if around it, on which side?

Brown went forward again, alone, limping out on reconnaissance to examine the various routes. To find out exactly where the danger lay, he walked in the most exposed places so the Germans would fire at him. Two machine-gun bullets cracked into him, and he fell. Fortunately he was not killed. This was the thirteenth time Bobbie Brown had been wounded in World War II.

He went back to his company. Again a medic approached, but Brown pushed him away gently. "Haven't time," he said. "These wounds have stopped bleeding." He formed his company, placed it on the best route up the hill, walked slowly up in front of the scouts so he could act as a guide, and beckoned the company to come on.

Crucifix Hill fell to Brown and his men forty minutes later, but for the next six hours Brown worked to make certain that the Germans could not retake the position. He checked the locations of each of his company's weapons, made sure that they had the best possible field of fire, that the defense was coördinated, that his men were in the safest places, that they had ammunition, and that food was brought up. Then Brown limped back to examine the three pillboxes he had dynamited. In them he found five wounded Germans and the remains of sixty-seven others. Back with his company on the other side of the hill, Brown lay down and allowed his wounds to be treated. "I am tired," he said.

Bobbie Brown's heroism helped part of the First United States Army to capture the important city of Aachen in the Siegfried Line. His superman performance, like the deeds of other heroes in this book, won him the Medal of Honor. Today Brown is retired and works at West Point, New York, in a civilian capacity. When he wears his uniform on special occasions, his left breast is graced by the coveted, light-blue ribbon that bears five tiny white stars, signifying that his deed at Crucifix Hill was above and beyond the call of duty.

14

FRED CASTLE
at the Battle of the Bulge

In western Europe in late December, 1944, Field Marshal Karl von Rundstedt poured all the German troops he could spare into one last all-out assault against the weakest part of the Allied battle lines. He was gambling on speed for a clean breakthrough to the port of Antwerp. If he succeeded he would split the Allied forces in two and close off a valuable source of supply, thus thwarting the rapid Allied advance into Germany.

South of Liège, Belgium, the Germans penetrated to a depth of fifty miles. Allied reinforcements rushed to plug the gap, and a great deal of fierce fighting took place. The press called it The Battle of the Bulge.

For the Allies, the situation looked somber. Rarely did General Eisenhower write one of his Orders of the Day. But three days before Christmas he sent out the message, "We can turn the enemy's great gamble into his worst defeat. So I call upon every man to rise now to new heights of courage, resolution, and effort . . ." For every Allied soldier, Eisenhower's message was the guide light.

Far back of the lines in England, senior generals in the United States Strategic Air Force readied 2,032 heavy bombers to strike for the hard-pressed Allied ground troops. For two years the United States Eighth Air Force had been pounding German rail centers, manufacturing districts, hydroelectric stations, bridges, dams, and other key installations. But this new raid was to include the largest number of bombers the world had ever seen.

The young officer selected to lead this force had risen from the rank of captain to brigadier general in two years. He was Brigadier General Fred Castle— quiet, restless, and unusual. The men in the Eighth Air Force liked him because he was alert and informal. Castle came to their mess halls and ate with them. The men knew he was interested in them and that he also was eager to hear their ideas. He wanted faster ways of gassing planes, more potent systems for coördinating air strikes, and quicker methods of repairing planes damaged in combat. He was a genius at problem analysis, and his organizational ability helped build the Eighth Air Force into a tremendously effective fighting unit.

One night, shortly before the new mission, General Castle was working late in his office on papers related to the raid. An adjutant interrupted him to announce that there were callers outside whom the general would enjoy seeing. They were a group of the general's young friends, English boys from Bury Saint Edmunds, who occasionally came to see him. They liked General Castle because he always found time to see them and because his cheerful air was a kind of reassurance that soon the terrible war would end in victory. Castle told the boys that on December 25 he would give them a real, old-fashioned Christmas party.

On the day before Christmas Brigadier General Fred Castle walked to his plane. The pilots who saw him knew that great danger lay ahead, because General Castle always flew when the missions were the most hazardous. He flew when heavy *ack-ack* and concentrations of enemy fighters could be expected. The pilots who saw him told one another, "Rough mission coming up." After Castle's plane had taken off, the people tending the airdromes said to one another, "Castle's in the air."

Castle's awesome air armada, protected by 800 fighters, began assembling in the skies. It was about to take off on the greatest air strike anyone had ever envisioned. Fred Castle had 30-day leave orders in his pocket, but there was no thought of leave when Eisenhower's Order of the Day had reached Bury Saint Edmunds. B-17's and B-24's from all over England left their airfields and droned into position. Castle was in the lead B-17.

The Red and Blue squadrons were five hundred feet higher than the lead squadron, and high above the three bomber squadrons flew the fighters. The formation extended as far back as the eye could see. The target: German airdromes in the Ardennes.

At 22,000 feet, Castle and the nine members of his Flying Fortress crew were cold in spite of heavy jackets and fur-lined gloves. Down through the fuzzy, altostratus clouds, the English Channel looked like an irregular band of blue steel.

When his plane was over Belgium, General Castle checked the course over the intercom with his three navigators. Thirty-five miles ahead, at 120 degrees, black smoke floating upward marked the city of Liège. At a point slightly northeast of the city the flight would

divide into three groups which would bombard their respective targets.

Down on the ground, infantry and armored divisions of the First United States Army were hurrying into position to reinforce hard-pressed Allied troops against the onrushing Germans.

Suddenly, without warning, fire blazed from the right, out-wing motor of General Castle's plane. Its propeller spun to a stop, looking like a bleak sign post. The copilot shut down the number four engine and actuated "the fire bottle," but the motor continued to blaze.

Castle switched on the intercom so that each member of the crew could listen in on his orders. He called his second-in-command (in the plane just behind), the leaders of the other two bomber squadrons, and the commander of the fighters. His voice was crisp, but lacked any hint of panic. He said, "Purple Leader calling Purple Two, Red Leader, Blue Leader, and Rapier-Echo Eight. Lost number four engine. Purple Two take over and command mission. Will follow at

a lower altitude. Will try 20,000. Purple Two, acknowledge. Out!"

Castle dropped the big plane to 20,000 feet, but it vibrated badly. He pushed the nose of the Fortress downward again. At 17,000 feet the air speed fell to 180 miles per hour. When Fred Castle leveled the plane and rechecked with the navigators, the ball-turret gunner cut into the conversation and reported to the general that seven Messerschmidts were tailing the general's B-17.

Red tracer bullets darted by the wings of the Fortress. The radar navigator, strapped in his seat, slumped forward over his table. Blood spurted from four wounds in his neck and shoulders. The tail gunner announced over the intercom, "General, I am wounded."

The Messerschmidts split. Three of them made passes at the disabled bomber from a 90-degree angle; the other three circled and attacked again from the rear. The B-17 could not try evasive tactics because of its heavy load of bombs and gasoline. Two other

engines caught fire.

The B-17 floundered. General Castle would not jettison his bombs because of the men of the First United States Army below. It would be disastrous to let the bombs fall on American infantrymen.

Castle wrestled with the controls to keep the plane level. The plane shook as if it were coming apart. He snapped over the intercom, "This is it, men. Bail out!"

The crew chief opened the door and the wind slammed into the plane. The regular pilot appeared at the door and shouted to Major Paul Biri, young bombardier navigator from New Orleans, Louisiana, "I can't find my parachute."

"It's probably in the cockpit," Biri shouted. At that moment Biri's hair caught fire and he jumped and floated safely to the ground.

At 12,000 feet the Messerschmidts roared back. Their bullets set the fuel tanks and oxygen systems of the crippled plane on fire. Castle's Flying Fortress looked like a flaming coffin. The Messerschmidts turned their machine guns on the men in the parachutes.

Castle guided the plane toward an open field where it would not injure American infantrymen. Near the ground, the plane went into a spin. It crashed with the noise of the explosion of an atomic cannon.

Infantrymen rushed to the site, but there was nothing they could do. They found two burned bodies in the wrecked plane. The charred body at the controls bore identification tags reading, FRED W. CASTLE, BRIG. GEN., USAF.

That night, General Carl Spaatz, Strategic Air Force commander, called Washington on the transatlantic telephone and gave General Henry H. Arnold, chief of the United States Air Forces, the sad news of Fred Castle's death. The Eighth Air Force had helped the ground forces, but at the cost of a fearless pilot, a top leader.

Later General Arnold was responsible for the naming of an Air Force field near Fresno, California, in Fred Castle's honor. The dedication was attended by national, state, and Air Force officers, by Major Paul Biri, and by Castle's father and mother. A few months later, at Mountain Lakes, New Jersey, Lieutenant General Ira Eaker, commander of the Eighth Air Force, spoke at a most impressive ceremony, telling how Fred Castle fearlessly laid down his life for men he did not know. Then General Eaker presented the Medal to Fred's mother, Mrs. Winifred W. Castle. A bugler blew taps, and relatives and friends bowed their heads in memory of a distinguished human being.

At West Point, where Fred Castle had been an outstanding cadet at the United States Military Academy, his Medal of Honor is displayed in a rotunda of Thayer Hall as an inspiration to future leaders of ground and air forces. When a portrait of General Castle was unveiled at West Point, General Eaker, again the principal speaker, said, "Fred Castle stands forever in the front ranks of gallant men."

PART THREE

The War in Korea
1950-1953

15

BILL DEAN,
Combat General

When the hostilities of World War II ended in September, 1945, most of the world expected peace, although affairs in the Far East were far from settled. The problem of Korea loomed, even though the Allies, at the conferences of 1943 and 1945, had pledged eventual independence for that country. Russia, too, had endorsed this pledge just before the war ended.

After the Japanese surrender, as a matter of convenience, it was agreed among the Americans, the British, and the Russians that the 38th Parallel would become a boundary between North and South Korea. This Parallel runs across the approximate center of the country. Japanese soldiers north of the Parallel were to surrender to the Russians, those south of it to the United States.

But as soon as possible, the Russians began organizing North Korea into another Communist satellite state. Americans were shocked when, on June 25, 1950, an army of North Koreans equipped with Soviet tanks and aircraft crashed across the 38th Parallel into South Korea.

The great powers of the United Nations, with the exception of Russia, joined to repel the hordes from the north, but the brunt of the fighting was borne by South Korea and the United States. General Douglas MacArthur, who was in Japan, was designated commander in chief for the United Nations, and he rushed three American divisions to Korea, the "Land of the Morning Calm."

The first American soldiers to land in Korea after the Communists slashed across the parallel were those of the 24th Infantry Division, led by a rangy six-footer with a wry grin and bushy eyebrows that gave him a fierce appearance and concealed his sense of humor. The two stars of a major general graced his collar. This was Major General William F. "Bill" Dean, of Berkeley, California—a modest individual and one of the most popular officers in the United States Army. He had the respect of every one of his soldiers.

He and his men found the situation chaotic. There were hundreds of rumors about the enemy, but little precise information. No one knew exactly where the enemy's strength lay. The South Koreans were fighting well in the mountains near Taejon, but they were handicapped by their ancient aircraft, by a lack of trained pilots, and by artillery that was outranged. Throngs of pitiful refugees choked the roads. Many of these were grandfathers, grandmothers, mothers carrying babies on their backs, and children. Carts and automobiles of every description crawled along. Tucked away in them were the infirm and the sick. The refugees heard the guns in the mountains and the Soviet jets in the skies. But even though the sounds of war were all about them, the pitiful columns continued to snail along.

As soon as General Dean set up his headquarters near Taejon, South Korean politicians bothered him by asking favors and by telling him how to fight. They described the enemy that Dean and his 10,000 men were up against, but no two agreed on how many North Koreans had swarmed across the border. The immediate future looked bleak, but Dean had a fighting plan.

He decided that his only chance was to have his men crash into the Communists, then retreat slowly, fighting all the way. He planned to make the enemy pay for every inch they gained, until more American soldiers could be brought in from Japan, Okinawa, Hawaii, and the United States. Soldiers were also coming from other U.N. countries: Australia, New Zealand, Canada, England, Holland, and Turkey.

Like the men at Wake Island, Dean wondered how

soon help would arrive. He knew his men were handicapped because they would have to fight with out-of-date bazookas and light tanks and light mortars against the modern weapons of the enemy.

Dean's division attacked and, for a moment, stopped the Communists, but the Americans were badly outnumbered. Hundreds of men in General Dean's command were killed or wounded.

Dean ranged up and down the barren, knifelike ridges, constantly encouraging his men. But it was disheartening, exhausting work. Many American youths

who, back home, had been used to riding almost everywhere in automobiles found that their legs would not stand the strain of climbing Korean mountains. Dean himself weighed 210 pounds, but he was soon down to 170, his weight when he was a young man earning money by stevedoring on the San Francisco docks to pay his way at the University of California.

The pressure on the United States forces was tremendous. Colonel Guy S. Meloy, a top regimental commander, was almost captured when he was wounded alongside his men, but his soldiers saved him by carrying him to the rear in a tank.

The fighting became even more confused as more Communists entered the battle. To make matters worse, inexperienced U.N. aviators bombed General Dean and his men. Had the 24th Division been commanded by a general of lesser spirit it would probably have fallen apart on the second day it met the Communist hordes.

In the battle, an infantry general remains at his headquarters most of the time so he can control the fight, although the great generals have made themselves available at times so their men may see them. The colonels and other officers are trained to discover enemy intentions, evaluate them, and send reports back to the general. He and his staff consider every aspect of the situation: the enemy's position, the men who are available, the help that may be expected from the artillery and from the air, communications, transportation, supplies on hand, and medical arrangements. When the general makes up his mind, with the advice of his staff, the plan is sent to the colonels, who follow it in detail.

On the twentieth day of the fight in South Korea, Dean's soldiers were almost beaten. The casualties of the 24th Division, and the superiority of the enemy, made Dean feel that he was of little use at his headquarters. He decided to add personally what force he could and to go down fighting.

It was 6:00 A.M. on a July day. Not a wisp of air stirred the azalea bushes alongside the headquarters. The red Korean sun peeping over a humpback ridge chased a blue mist from the valley and raised the temperature up into the nineties. The humid air made the uniforms clammy. General Dean buckled on his pistol and walked through the headquarters building, with its dirty thatched roof, to First Lieutenant Arthur Clarke. Nodding to Clarke and a South Korean interpreter, Jimmy Kim, the general said tersely, "Come on. Let's go tank hunting."

Clarke and Kim picked up their carbines and followed the strapping general over the mountains to Taejon. Smoke was rising above the town. Some of Dean's men were in the city, but they had little chance

because the enemy tanks were crashing through the homes and were pounding all opposition with heavy cannon.

A tank bulldozed through a ruined home and rumbled down the street toward Dean and his two friends. Fortunately the driver in the "buttoned up" tank did not see them. Dean, at the end of his patience, whipped out his .45 pistol and fired a clip at the monster. The tank clanked on, the people in it not knowing they were being fired at.

Dean found an American bazooka man close by and told him to join the group with his tank-killing weapon. The general started to lead his three men through a courtyard, but North Korean infantrymen protecting other tanks fired at them and stopped the little group. Bill Dean decided that if he and the bazooka man could get upstairs in a nearby building they would be safe from the enemy riflemen and might be able to wreck a tank by firing through the tank's roof, which was not armored as thickly as its sides.

The general pulled himself up onto the window ledge of a vacant house and clambered in, his men close behind. The abandoned house had an acid smell. Bullets had ripped through a movable screen that separated two upstairs living rooms. On a bamboo table sat a yellow dish, on a white doily, holding a bunch of violets.

The explosion of an enemy shell wrecked the next

house, and bits of thatched roof rained down on the four men. On the street below a Communist tank squatted, its guns raking the area. It was hard to talk above the noise. General Dean placed the bazooka man by the window and pointed at the tank, less than fifteen feet away.

The blast of the bazooka shook the building. North Koreans in the tank screamed again and again. Bill Dean, a kindly man but under great pressure because of the slaughter of his men and the unbelievable cruelty of the enemy, cried, "Hit them again!"

After the tank had been knocked out, Dean, back in his headquarters, decided that the only thing he could do to delay the enemy was to form a task force of every available man. Rounding up clerks, cooks, kitchen police, spare truck drivers, mechanics, messengers, musicians, and military policemen, he led them back into town in a desperate do-or-die attack, but in the end they were beaten back.

There was no hope of gathering the remnants of the task force, so Dean and Clarke walked through the ruined town to its southern edge. At a road junction they helped a few doctors and first-aid men care for the wounded. A warning came that the enemy would soon arrive, but Dean worked to load the wounded in trucks until it was obvious that if he stayed any longer he would be captured. He and Lieutenant Clarke climbed into a jeep, after the trucks had departed, and dashed through a lane lined on both sides by enemy snipers. Dean aided the escape of the jeep by shooting rapid fire at the snipers with an M-1 rifle. Enemy tanks lumbered after them but could not keep up with the jeep.

On its way south the jeep took a wrong turn, and its occupants became lost—separated from the rest of the division. Turning around and going back was impossible because of enemy tanks, so Dean and Clarke abandoned the jeep and walked across the barren country.

At night, the two friends became separated. General Dean spent thirty-five lonely, exhausting days in the mountains trying to get back to the Americans. He lived on uncooked grain and celery roots; occasionally a friendly South Korean farmer gave him a meal of cooked rice. Everywhere the general turned he found the enemy. He now traveled at night, armed only with his pistol and twelve rounds, one of which he determined to save for himself.

News that General Dean was missing flashed around the world. General Earle Partridge of the United States Air Force, and other aviators, flew long hours in light planes searching for him, without success.

Finally, two Koreans came upon the American general. Pretending to be friendly, they slyly arranged for his capture. South Korean police said later that the pair received the equivalent of five dollars for turning General Dean over to the Communists.

The North Koreans threw Dean in a cage and kept him like an animal. For three years he was their prisoner in filthy prison camps. For long months guards made him remain on the floor, allowing him to exercise only at night. He kept himself from going crazy by performing mathematical problems in his head and by trying to kill more flies each day than he had the day before. Dean said that one of the happiest days of his life was in the sixteenth month of his captivity when his guards finally granted his request for a pencil and paper so he could write his wife, Mildred.

Finally a cease-fire agreement was arranged, and an uneasy peace settled between North and South Korea. But still the Communists were in no hurry to let General Dean go, although they themselves had received prisoners returned by the U.N. command. At last, on September 3, 1953—thirty-eight days after the two sides reached an agreement on terms for a truce— General Dean was repatriated.

When Bill Dean returned he was almost a skeleton, but his physique, his indomitable spirit, and expert

medical care brought back his health. He was surprised
to learn that his wife had received for him the Medal
of Honor from President Truman. Dean said that he
was humbly grateful for the wonderful honor, but
that others had done better jobs and received no
recognition.

Three years later the South Korean police arrested
the two men who had betrayed General Dean. Dean
wrote to President Rhee of Korea saying that pun-
ishing them would accomplish nothing, but one of
them was put to death and the other was sentenced to
imprisonment for life.

Today the popular and modest general lives in
Berkeley, California, and is active in raising funds for
the American Cancer Society and the Boy Scouts of
America. The American survivors of those difficult
days at the outset of the Korean War were pleased that
Dean received the Medal. His fight and survival
against tremendous odds is a testament of the American
spirit.

16

MELVIN BROWN,
Fighting Engineer

Two months after General Dean had been reported missing, a Medal of Honor was won in Korea in a most unusual way. The situation of the U.N. forces was desperate. The Communists of North Korea had hammered them backward to the southeast end of the country, into a corner of the peninsula measuring 70 by 100 miles. The Allies dubbed this area "The Pusan Perimeter," and the world waited to see if the U.N. army would be pushed into the sea.

In the battle lines, the United States had only approximately 45,000 men, not enough to form a backbone of a strong U.N. army. On the same debit side of the ledger, United States soldiers were armed with weapons of World War II vintage—not as good as those of the enemy—and there was a scarcity of ammunition.

In the fall of 1950, about the only thing that General MacArthur could be proud of was the fact that the United States soldiers were fighting their hardest. This was evidenced at the "Walled City," near Taegu, about eighty miles up from the southern tip of the Korean peninsula.

The situation was so grim there that Major General Hobart Gay, commanding the 1st Cavalry Division, not only placed his reserve—the combat engineers—in the line, but he reinforced them with cooks, messengers, truck drivers, and everyone else he could find, just as General Dean had done at Taejon. One of the combat engineers at the Walled City was a young soldier from Mahaffey, Pennsylvania—Melvin L. Brown.

In the United States Army, the combat engineers are carefully trained men. Sometimes they are referred to as "pioneer troops" because at times they perform a variety of jobs such as constructing and repairing bridges, and building heliports, defense positions, roads, and railroad track. They are trained to operate heavy construction equipment, and can lay deadly mines and demolitions. This is the engineering side of their training. The other side is even more important, for when there is a dire emergency they may be rushed to the crucial point on the battlefield and employed as infantry reserves.

Melvin Brown was a member of an old organization, the 1st Cavalry Division. Long ago the division had been mounted on horses, but in Korea it was fighting on foot. Brown, like every soldier in the division, wore its peculiar shoulder patch, shaped like a shield of a medieval knight. It has the golden-yellow color of the setting sun on a Texas prairie. Its black stripe represents service, and its horse's head the devotion of the old-time cavalrymen to their mounts.

Brown was a private first class, and although he was not the leader of a unit, he was a daredevil. Later, looking back, Master Sergeant James Vandygriff, also a combat engineer, said that mild-looking, narrow-jawed Melvin Brown was not one to care about his personal safety.

Although the 1st Cavalry Division was stretched thin —7,000 riflemen holding a front of nearly 60 miles— it readied itself to battle the oncoming Communists.

Its 8th Engineer Battalion found itself assigned a section of the last-ditch defense line at the peculiar Walled City. Behind the men, in the twisted mountains, rose a sharp granite peak, 3,900 feet high. The South Koreans called it "Sacred Mountain," but on the maps of the officers it was labeled "Hill 855." There was no city, but on the lonely, sloping plateau stood a forlorn Buddhist temple.

First Sergeant Connie L. Adams, artilleryman, has described the place. "The temple looked like a run-down castle that at one time probably had five roofs, one on top of the other. But what took my eye was the wall along the edge of the drop-off. The wall—it was crumbled and wasn't too good in places—was used in the old days to keep out the war lords. In some spots it was about 40 feet high, in others about 5 feet. The wall looked like a stone belt gripping the edge of the mile-long crest."

Melvin Brown's platoon sergeant, John J. Philip, placed his weary engineers behind the wall and told them to dig in. Young Brown and his friend, Private Herman Schildmeyer, dug their foxholes 20 yards apart. It was hard digging; the points of their entrenching shovels struck rock every few inches. But the engineers were spurred on because in the distance smoke rose from the large railroad yards at Waegwan, about 5 miles away and already in Communist hands. Every engineer had been warned that there was nothing in front of the wall to stop the enemy.

When most of the foxholes were completed, there was a mail delivery from Japan, where the wives of Brown and some of the others were living. For two hours the men had time to rest from their labors in the September heat and eat emergency rations of canned stew, chocolate, and raisin bars. A few of the men walked to the old temple, where they relaxed under the scrub pines on brown pine needles. The scene looked peaceful except for the smoke drifting

up beyond the mountains. The country could have been part of the Adirondacks in New York State. It was hard to believe the area was dangerous.

By dusk the area was dead quiet, except for the click of a few entrenching shovels. Then suddenly rifle fire cracked out far to the left, where 1st Cavalry infantrymen were fighting "civilians" dressed in blue cotton trousers and white shirts like those worn by the peasants. The civilians were armed with rifles and were attacking. This was an enemy trick. The men in civilian clothing were North Koreans who hoped to catch the Americans unaware.

In the dim light, Communists in civilian clothing and in North Korean uniforms scrambled up the hills to the right of the wall like mountain goats, carrying machine guns and ammunition on their backs.

At three in the morning machine-gun bullets whined down the wall, and Brown and other engineers ducked into their foxholes. The bullets showered the Americans with granite chips from the wall and ricocheted off into the air with a high-pitched whine.

The engineers shot flares into the air, illuminating the place with a greenish-white glare so they could see their attackers. The Communists had an advantage; they knew the Americans were along the wall.

In spite of the machine-gun bullets, Brown and other engineers left their foxholes and took places at the wall, where they could fire their rifles better.

Brown emptied his M-1 at forms sprinting toward the wall. One moment the enemy soldiers looked real;

then after the flares had faded and before others could be sent up, they looked like shadows.

An M-1 rifle eats up ammunition, and soon Brown and his squad leader had nothing but empty clips. Brown called to his sergeant for more, just as a machine-gun slug bit a chunk of flesh out of his arm. Parachute flares and flares fired from signal pistols disclosed that the North Koreans were rushing Brown's part of the wall in greater numbers, and the back ranks carried scaling ladders. Would the American engineers ever be able to hold fast?

Brown begged for more bullets, but there were none to spare. His friends tossed him hand grenades, which he caught like a baseball player. He pulled the safety cotter pins and threw the grenades down into the Communists in spite of the pain he was suffering. Enemy soldiers screamed, others tried to climb the wall.

Some engineers, like Brown, were at the wall. Others were in their foxholes waiting for the North Koreans to appear over the wall. In the weird light Brown saw men on the scaling ladders, and others who were inching their way up the wall by gripping it with their fingers and toes. Brown reached for his shovel.

When a Communist head came in view, Brown brought his entrenching shovel down on it with all his might. In spite of the blood spurting from his wound, he ran along the wall hitting every head that appeared.

The enemy, however, continued to swarm over the wall at the place where Brown fought. What happened to the brave engineer, no one knows. His platoon, inspired by his fierce fight, attacked and recaptured their segment of the wall, but they could not find Private Melvin Brown. Perhaps he fell over the wall and was carried away; the odds are that he died fighting. At daybreak, the bodies piled up at the bottom of the wall beneath the spot where Brown had fought were grim evidence of his amazing and unwavering fight.

At West Point, during the Korean War, it was customary for the cadet adjutant to read the citations for the Medal of Honor to the Corps of Cadets after the publication of orders in the huge cadet dining hall. The cadets stood at attention in respect for the men who won the Medal. After Brown's citation was read, each cadet bowed his head in silent prayer for a man who did not know what it was to quit.

17

BILLIE KANELL
of the Golden Rule

The fight at the Walled City had been over for nine days when General MacArthur surprised the Communists in Korea by landing fresh U.S. troops behind the enemy lines on the east coast at Inchon. This smart move cut the principal north supply routes of the enemy and made possible the recapture of Seoul, the capital—a city that means much to every Korean.

Completely surprised, the Communists fled northward up the peninsula, and MacArthur's men followed them as fast as they could. When his U.N. command neared the border between Manchuria and North Korea, the Western world received a shock; approximately 150,000 soldiers of Communist China swarmed across the Yalu River, with Russian approval, and attacked. This happened in mid-October, 1950. By the end of November 150,000 more Chinese Communist forces were across the Yalu battling the outnumbered U.N. soldiers.

The Chinese proved to be excellent fighters, accustomed to hardship. They quickly discovered that Americans could be upset by night attacks and by combat patrols which attacked in the rear areas. For months the fighting raged, with the U.N. forces slowly being pushed back.

In September, 1951, there was especially hard fighting at the "Iron Triangle," an open plateau covering about seventy-five square miles, which lay sixty miles north of Seoul. The Iron Triangle contained important road junctions. Although truce talks were being conducted between the two armies, both sides were scrambling for the best positions, trying to obtain them by combat. Much of this was close-in fighting, with the Communists hurling their peculiar "potato masher" hand grenades.

The soldiers of the 35th Infantry Regiment of the 25th Infantry Division were in hasty defensive positions, two to four men to a hole. The foxholes pitted the ridge tops and formed the irregular line the Chinese were attacking. In one of the dank, smelly holes, Private Billie Gene Kanell stood with two

friends. September of 1951 was a time when the defenders needed all the courage they could muster to stay in position.

Kanell was only 5 feet 4 inches tall, but he had the courage of a lion. Back in Poplar Bluff, Missouri, a pleasant town on the low bluffs of the Black River in the foothills of the Ozarks, Billie Kanell had grown up with eight brothers and sisters. He was small for athletics. Because he was also troubled with bad knees, he kept himself busy in his spare time by reading every book he could find and by working to help others.

Billie's mother, Mrs. Iva Walker Kanell, taught her children to assist one another with work about the house and to be very thoughtful of others.

After Kanell graduated from the Eugene Field Grade School and the Poplar Bluff Senior High School, the Communists from North Korea crashed into South Korea. The free world was under attack. Billie Kanell, nineteen years old, kissed his mother, sisters, and brothers good-by, quit the job he liked—tree surgery in the Ozarks—and volunteered.

He was a success at once. The soldiers liked his soft drawl, and they sought his companionship because he helped everyone he could. Private Kanell was one of the most popular men in his company.

In the early hours of the lonely, misty morning of September 7, the quiet of the Iron Triangle was shattered by the Communists. It was dark. Kanell and two friends, Privates First Class F. M. Rodriguez and Stephen Mullan, were under special attack because, the day before, the Chinese had located the Browning automatic rifle in their rifle pit. But Rodriguez, with the help of Kanell and Mullan, swept the down-slope with bullets. The rapid fire of the automatic was a barrier the Chinese could not crack.

Artillery and mortar fire crashed down in the darkness on the Americans. The bursting shells blazed red and white as they deluged the ridge with sharp scraps of iron. Some men in the foxholes were killed and others were wounded, but Rodriguez, Mullan, and Kanell survived.

As soon as the mortar and artillery fire ceased, Americans all along the line shot flares into the air in the hope of locating the enemy. The three friends fired their weapons at the shadowy forms that were crawling closer to their foxhole, but it was hard to aim in the uncertain light.

The Chinese threw hand grenades, and one burst not far away. The three men flinched as mud and stones rained on them.

Like all American soldiers, they hated Communist grenades, not only because hand-grenade fire meant that the enemy was within throwing range, but because the Chinese hand grenades had erratic fuses. Sometimes they would burst within three seconds after being

thrown. At other times, twenty-five seconds would pass before the grenade would explode and hurl its iron fragments over a 33-foot radius. It was impossible to judge the length of time it would take a grenade to explode after landing.

As daylight etched the Korean mountains against a blue-gray sky, unseen Chinese peppered the men of Company I, 35th Infantry, with grenade fragments. The flat, awful cough of the grenades echoed continually up and down the ridge.

Suddenly an enemy grenade plunked into the mud of Kanell's foxhole, between Kanell and his two friends. All three saw the black potato masher. They were trapped. Before the grenade could explode and tear his friends apart, Kanell dove for it. The instant he covered the grenade with his body, it exploded, ripping a hole in his side.

Rodriguez and Mullan yelled. From the nearest foxhole, 15 yards away, two more of Kanell's friends, Ronald Johnston and Raymond Jahner, rushed to them. They saw Kanell, white-faced but alive, on the muddy floor, with blood pouring from his wound.

Another grenade arced through the air and thumped into the mud between Kanell and Rodriguez.

Before anyone else could move, Kanell summoned his fast-waning strength and rolled himself over on the second grenade, covering it and absorbing its explosion.

Later, when the awful telegram to his parents arrived at Poplar Bluff, announcing Kanell's death, his family was numb from the dreadful shock. His mother wrote, "My soul died that evening."

Kanell's body was brought home, and a memorial service was held in the Methodist Church where he had worshiped. Shortly afterwards, the Kanell family traveled to Washington to receive the Medal from Secretary of the Army, Frank Pace, Jr.

The United States named a rifle and pistol range on the southern skirts of Seoul *Kanell Range,* and placed a bronze plaque at a prominent place on the range, where it can be read by United States soldiers and soldiers of South Korea. The plaque describes Kanell's sacrifice and tells that he was awarded the Medal of Honor posthumously.

When the range was dedicated, Chaplain John Rhea, a colonel in the United States Army, stood in front of dignitaries and soldiers gathered to honor Kanell's memory. The chaplain told the story of Billie Kanell's sacrifice and prayed that God would give every American the courage of the great citizen and soldier who had lived by the Golden Rule, even to the point of giving his life for his friends.

A Shrine
for the Medal

Like the precious laurel wreath that was bestowed
long ago upon heroes of the Mediterranean countries,
the Medal of Honor, awarded to heroic Americans, is
symbolic of the respect of the people of the United
States. The heroism of the winners of the Medal is
part of the nation's heritage. Only the bravest of the
brave and those most dedicated to their fellow men
can win this decoration. The heroes of the Medal of
Honor are enshrined forever in the hearts of their
countrymen.

To insure a physical shrine for men of the Medal,
Dr. Kenneth Wells, president of Freedoms Foundation
in Valley Forge, Pennsylvania, had plans drawn up
in 1964 for the creation of a Medal of Honor Grove at
Valley Forge. Fifty-two acres of hills and streams,
hallowed by early patriots of the Revolutionary War,
have been set aside, one section for each of the fifty

states, Puerto Rico, and the District of Columbia. Each section will contain a monument to the state, special tablets to its Medal winners, and a living tree to mark in perpetuity each recipient of the Medal. Boy Scouts of America have already dedicated trees in the grove to former Boy Scouts who won the Medal.

Medal of Honor records are hard to come by. They are buried, scattered, and sometimes guarded. But in the future all books and other available records pertaining to these heroic deeds will be assembled at the shrine. To obtain the huge amount of money needed for this establishment, Freedoms Foundation appointed a special committee of prominent and influential Americans, headed by a retired four-star general, Bruce C. Clarke. The aim of his committee is to establish a great national shrine of impelling significance to all Americans.

Author's Note

It required three years for me to assemble the data and record these accounts of twentieth century heroes who received the Medal of Honor. During this time I was often asked, "Why did you select these particular winners of the Medal?" Three of the men I know. Their lives and deeds almost demanded that I write their stories. The rest I selected to show the variety of the service of Medal winners.

Though I would like to acknowledge here, individually, all those who helped with this book, such an exhaustive roster would tend to overbalance the book. Therefore, the reader will find here only the names of those whose assistance helped me in telling one or more of these stories in considerable detail. I am truly grateful for all the coöperation I received, and that includes all those who furnished information or who helped by performing errands. The following winners of the Medal of Honor contributed: Bobbie E. Browne, Robert E. Bush, William F. Dean, Edouard V. M. Izac, Robert G. Robinson, Oscar Schmidt, and Louis Van Iersel.

The suggestion for a book about Medal heroes came from Mrs. Lavinia Russ of New York City. Supporting the idea, wrestling with the manuscript, and aiding me at every turn was my wife, Dort Darrah Reeder, my private editor, expert typist, and keen copy reader.

The book also benefited by coöperation from the following who were close to Medal of Honor holders, or who have intimate knowledge of action surrounding the winning of a Medal, or who contributed key information: First Sergeant Connie L. Adams; Major Paul L. Biri, survivor of Fred Castle's last flight; Commander George E. Brown, survivor of the last cruise of the U.S. Submarine *Sculpin;* Colonel Benjamin F. Castle; Lieutenant Colonel D. M. Cooney; Rear Admiral Tom Hamilton; Brigadier General Harris B. Hull; Mrs. J. W. Kanell; Major General J. C. Lambert; Robert B. Lea; Brigadier General Frank McCarthy; David C. "Spec" McClure, who twice toured the battlefields of France with Audie Murphy; Mrs. Betty Pruitl; Rear Admiral Fred M. Reeder; Father Martin E. Ryan, S.J.; The Selectmen of the Town of South Weymouth, Mass.; Lieutenant J. W. Stierman, U.S.N.; John O. Talbot; Colonel Charles C.

Underwood; and Major General George V. "Bud" Underwood, Jr.

I appreciate receiving permission from Random House, Inc., to use a paper that aviators of the First World War dropped to fighters on the ground. This paper is from *Memoirs of World War I* by Brigadier General William Mitchell; copyright, 1960 by Lucy M. Gilpin; copyright, 1928, by *Liberty* Weekly, Inc.; copyright, 1956, by Lorraine Lester and Associates.

I am also extremely grateful for invaluable assistance by The National Archives and especially by The Department of Defense.

Red Reeder

West Point,
New York.

Bibliography

The Medal of Honor of the United States Army, Public
Information Division, Department of the Army, 1948.
*Medal of Honor, U. S. Bureau of Naval Personnel, 1861–
1949,* Department of the Navy, 1950.

Boswell, Rolfe, *Leathernecks; Our Marines in Fact and
Picture,* N.Y.: Thos. Y. Crowell Co., 1934.
Craven, Avery O., and Johnson, Walter, *American History,*
N.Y.: Ginn and Co., 1961.
Cunningham, Winfield Scott, and Sims, Lydel, *Wake
Island Command,* Boston: Little, Brown & Co., 1961.
Esposito, Vincent J., Col. (editor), *The West Point Atlas
of American Wars,* N.Y.: Frederick A. Praeger.
Dean, William F., Maj. Gen., *General Dean's Story,* N.Y.:
The Viking Press, 1954.
Donovan, Frank, *The Medal,* N.Y.: Dodd Mead and Co.,
1962.
Heinl, Robert D., Lt. Col., *The Defense of Wake,* U.S.
Marine Corps, 1947.

——*Soldiers of the Sea; the U.S. Marine Corps, 1775–1962,* Annapolis, Md., U.S. Naval Institute, 1962.

Jacobs, Bruce, *Heroes of the Army,* N.Y.: W. W. Norton and Co., 1956.

Janes Fighting Ships, 1919, N.Y.: McGraw-Hill, Inc

Jones, H. A., *The War in the Air; Being the Story of the Part Played in the Great War by The Royal Air Force,* vol. VI; Oxford, at the Clarendon Press, 1937.

Knox, Dudley W., *A History of the U.S. Navy,* N.Y.: G. P. Putnam's Sons, 1963.

Metcalf, Clyde H., *A History of the United States Marine Corps,* N.Y.: G. P. Putnam's Sons, 1939.

——*The Marine Corps Reader,* N.Y.: G. P. Putnam's Sons, 1944.

Mitchell, William B., Brig. Gen., *Memoirs of World War I,* N.Y.: Random House, 1960.

Montross, Lyn, *The United States Marines,* N.Y.: Rinehart and Co., 1959.

Morison, Samuel Eliot, *History of the U.S. Naval Operations in World War II,* Boston: Little, Brown & Co., 1947.

O'Callahan, Joseph Timothy, *I Was Chaplain on the Franklin,* N.Y.: Macmillan Co., 1956.

Pierce, Philip N., Lt. Col., and Hough, Frank O., Lt. Col., *The Compact History of the Marine Corps,* N.Y.: Hawthorne Books, Inc., 1964.

Pratt, Fletcher, *The Compact History of the U.S. Navy,* N.Y.: Hawthorne Books, 1962.

Robertson, Frederic Arthur de Vere, *Aircraft of the World,* London: H. Milford, 1924.

Sims, William Snowden, *The Victory at Sea,* N.Y.: Doubleday, Page and Co., 1920.

Spaulding, Oliver L., Col., and Wright, John W., Col., *The Second Division, American Expeditionary Force in France, 1917–1919,* N.Y.: The Hillman Press, Inc., 1937.

Stamps, T. Dodson, Col., and Esposito, Vincent J., Col., *A Short Military History of World War I,* West Point, 1950.

Sunderman, James F. (editor), *Early Air Pioneers, 1862–1935,* N.Y.: Franklin Watts, Inc., 1961.

Whitehouse, Arthur George Joseph, *The Years of the Sky Kings,* N.Y.: Doubleday and Co., 1959.

The Defense of Wake, The U.S. Marine Corps, Department of the Navy.

The Ninth U.S. Infantry in the World War (WWI; author, publisher, and year not recorded.)

About the Author

COLONEL RED REEDER, with his sister Nardi Reeder Campion, wrote the Landmark book THE WEST POINT STORY. He began his career as a writer in World War II when he was ordered by the Army's chief of staff, General George C. Marshall, to go to Guadalcanal and bring back the lessons that American soldiers and Marines were learning in leadership and in jungle warfare. Since then he has written twenty-four books, among them "the story of the war" series and the "Clint Lane" series, the latter about a boy at West Point.

When he was a cadet at West Point, Red Reeder played on the football and baseball teams. He graduated in 1926. In World War II he saw combat in New Guinea, Guadalcanal, and Normandy. In the invasion of Normandy he won the Distinguished Service Cross—and the Purple Heart. He is presently employed as Special Assistant to the Director of Athletics in the Army Athletic Association at West Point.

About the Illustrator

GIL WALKER has illustrated many books with military and historical backgrounds. Among them are *The Compact History of the United States Army, The Compact History of the United States Marine Corps, The Compact History of the Air Force,* and *The Compact History of the Coast Guard.*

A United States Army artist during World War II and the Korean War, Mr. Walker has also served as assistant art editor for *The Reporter* magazine. Now he is a regular contributor to such periodicals as *Harper's* magazine, *Boys' Life,* and *The Reporter,* as well as a popular illustrator of books for young readers.

Index